COMBAT ARMS

MODERN

SPYPLANES

DOUG RICHARDSON

PRENTICE
HALL
PRESS

NEW YORK • LONDON • TORONTO • SYDNEY • TOKYO • SINGAPORE

A Salamander Book

Prentice Hall Press
15 Columbus Circle
New York, New York 10023

An Arco Military Book

PRENTICE HALL PRESS and colophons are registered trademarks of Simon & Schuster, Inc.

Originally published in the United Kingdom by Salamander Books Ltd, 129-137 York Way, London N7 9LG.

Library of Congress Catalog Card Number 90-52990.

ISBN 0-13-589854-4

10 9 8 7 6 5 4 3 2 1

First Prentice Hall Press Edition

Credits

Editor: Richard Collins.
Designer: Mark Holt.
Color artwork: ©Salamander Books Ltd. and ©Pilot Press Ltd.
Filmset by The Old Mill, London.
Color reproduction: Track Origination.
Printed in Belgium by: Proost International Book Production, Turnhout.

The Author

Doug Richardson is a defense journalist and author specialising in the fields of aviation, guided missiles and electronics. After a successful career as an electronics and aerospace engineer he moved into journalism. He has been the Defense Editor of *Flight International*, Editor of *Military Technology*, and Editor of *Defense Material* before becoming a full-time freelance writer.

Contents

"MISSED Nivelles, but arrived at a big town, but could not place it on my map (On my return, I discovered this to have been Brussels) . . . picked up my position at Ottignes, and soon found Gembloux, after being in clouds I made a wide circle round, being in clouds part of the time, but saw only a small body of cavalry moving faster than a walk in a south-easterly direction."

This useless item of intelligence data was the sole result of the Royal Flying Corps' first reconnaissance mission of World War I, flown at 9.30am on 19 August 1914. For Lt Mapplebeck of No 4 Squadron, tackling this mission was largely a matter of grabbing a large scale and small scale map, choosing what he thought was the best aircraft (he opted for a BE.2a) then taking off in the company of a No 3 (F) Squadron Bleriot to deploy the only sensor he had, the Mk1 eyeball.

Less than a month later, a better sensor was used. On 15 September, Lt G. F. Petyman of No 3 Squadron used a camera he had brought to France to take five photos of German trenches. Even as the first official issue reconnaissance cameras entered service, the naked eye was to remain useful. Early cameras were fragile, and in short supply, and their installation within an aircraft was largely a matter of improvisation. By the spring of 1915, the custom-designed "A Type" recce camera was in service.

To the present day, the camera remains the most widely used sensor on reconnaissance aircraft, although current models bear little resemblance to their 1914-18 counterparts. The importance of traditional photographic film may decline in the 1990s, but the camera is here to stay.

Image quality is vital

Image quality from a reconnaissance camera depends on a number of factors, including the optical performance of the lens, the resolving power and contrast rendition of the film emulsion. External environmental factors such as light level, contrast conditions, and the amount of atmospheric haze also affect the quality of the images captured on film.

Some requirements of lenses are not too different from those demanded in conventional photography — high and evenly distributed image definition and contrast from the centre of the picture to its edge. Others are dictated by the fact that the photo-interpreter will use the image to estimate the size of objects on the ground. The lens must be essentially distortion free, and geometrically stable over a long period of use.

Anyone who has pointed a camera too close to the sun when taking a photo will be aware of how "flare" in the lens — solar reflections from the various glass surfaces — can ruin

Left: Early reconnaissance missions conducted during World War I were devoid of cameras; but they soon found their way into aircraft such as the RAF Be.2c.

Below: By the time World War II broke out, aerial reconnaissance cameras such as this F.24 used for oblique photography were bigger and better than their predecessors.

a photo. Photo missions are often flown with the sun low in the sky, so as to ensure good shadows, so the relative position of sun and target may not always be favourable. Good design is necessary if reflections are to be minimised.

Two factors have influenced camera design since World War II — the need to take recce photos first from high-altitude platforms, then from aircraft flying fast at very low altitude. High operating altitudes have dictated the need for lenses of longer focal length, while high speed operations at low altitude created the risk of blurring to terrain movement.

On the sort of camera widely used for photo-survey work, focal length can vary from 3.5in (8.8cm) (super-wide angle) to 12in (30cm) (normal). Move to high altitude, and longer focal lengths are needed if high resolution is to be obtained. These longer focal lengths provide photo-interpreters with the detailed imagery needed to scrutinise ground targets, but over a much smaller patch of terrain on each photo.

Focal length versus aircraft altitude

The problem is neatly illustrated by the brochure which NASA uses to publicise the services of its ER-2 (TR-1). From 65,000ft (19,812m) an RC-10 camera with a 6in (15cm) lens records a 16 × 16nm (29 × 29km) patch of terrain, the smallest details visible being between 9 and 26ft (3 and 8m). A 12in (30cm) lens improves the resolution to between 5 and 13ft (1.5 and 4m), but the terrain recorded on the film frame is only 8 × 8nm (14.8 × 14.8km). Substitute an HR-732 camera with a 24in (60cm) lens and the resolution rises to between 2 and 9ft (0.6 and 3m), while the 36in (91cm) lens of the HR-73B-1 manages between 1.6 and 6.5ft (0.5 and 2m). Use these long lenses, and you had better make sure the aircraft flies an accurate flight path. Each frame will record only 4 × 8nm (7.4 × 14.8km) and 5.3 × 5.3nm (9.8 × 9.8km) respectively.

The camera will almost certainly be mounted behind a window. This must be designed for minimal distortion or degradation of image quality. The glass should be chosen for high transmission, that is to say, minimal absorption of the incoming light, and is likely to be surfaced with an anti-reflective coating. If the aircraft or camera bay is pressurised, then the glass must be thick enough to withstand the difference in pressure between the interior and the outside atmosphere, typically 1.2-1.9in (3-5cm).

An earthbound photographer keen to obtain the highest possible definition will take care to hold the camera as steadily as possible, and may even opt to mount it on a tripod. Unfortunately, there are no tripods in the sky. The camera is moving at high speed, and is also subjected to the effects of turbulence (this takes the form of irregular rolling, pitching and yawing motions of the aircraft) and of aircraft vibration.

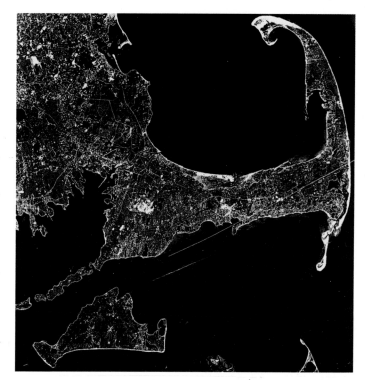

Above: An excellent example of the quality and resolution available from today's photo-reconnaissance equipment is provided in this view of part of England's south coast. The quality of such images depends on two primary factors: the focal length(s) of the camera lens(es) being utilised, and the altitude(s) from which the airborne platform housing the recce equipment is operating for the mission.

Aircraft motion creates problems

For many tactical purposes, photo-interpreters ideally want imagery with the largest possible scale. This can be achieved either by using a long focal length lens at high altitude, or a normal lens at low level. In both cases, this results in excessive image motion due to the forward velocity of the aircraft. Even during the brief fraction of a second needed to take the picture, the image cast on the film by the lens moves sufficiently to degrade the final photo. The lower sensitivity of high-resolution films requires longer exposure times which exacerbate the problem.

To overcome this, cameras are usually fitted with forward-motion compensation (FMC). This involves moving the film by the exact amount needed to offset the image movement caused by aircraft motion. Typical rates are between 0.04 and 2.5in/sec (1 and 64mm/sec).

A recent trend in camera design has been the incorporation of microprocessors to check camera functions, and ease the operator's workload. For example, the Wild Heerbrugg

Aviophot RC20 unit uses six microprocessors. The first controls and monitors all camera functions, the second and third deal with the shutter and aperture settings, also the cycling of operations needed to take a series of pictures. The fourth and sixth handle the projection of digital data onto the margin of the film (recording details of the camera, lens type, exposure settings, time between photos, position and altitude of aircraft, time, etc), and the fifth controls the FMC drive unit.

According to the manufacturer, the RC20 is also the first FMC aerial camera with an interface for direct connection to an aircraft navigation system such as the Litton LTN72 INS, Decca Doppler 72 TANS, Collins LRN-85 VLF/Omega system, or the Foster LNS 616/DI 681 Loran system. By linking the navigation system and camera, the correct amount of overlap between photos can be automatically obtained, while the accurately controlled flight path eliminates the risk of accidental gaps in the photo coverage.

The camera is only as good as the film used within it. Although similar in general concept to that used in normal cameras, film used for reconnaissance is normally 5in (2.5cm) wide and made from a base material of good dimensional stability. Photo-interpreters might not notice if their uniform were to shrink by a few per cent while being laundered, but when measuring the size of an image in order to deduce the dimensions of an object on the ground they need to be confident that the image has not been affected either by the film's immersion in processing solutions or by the stresses of mechanical handling. At the same time, the base material should be as thin as possible, to maximise the number of photos which can be taken with a single magazine of film.

Choosing the film

As any photographer knows, the resolving power of a film — that is to say its ability to record very fine detail — is inversely proportional to sensitivity. If maximum image detail is wanted, the photographer will select a "slow" (less sensitive) film, but if lighting conditions are poor, a "fast" (high-sensitivity) film will be able to capture an image, but the definition will be degraded. The less sensitive film will also produce a more contrasty image for the same lighting conditions than a "faster" film would.

An instance which takes these rules to the extreme is microfilming of documents. The film used tends to be very "slow", but offers high resolution and excellent contrast — exactly the qualities needed to capture a line drawing or page of text.

These same general rules also apply to film used for recce purposes. Where maximum image resolution is needed, the film will be at least two times slower than that of a typical aerial film. This is often the case with some of the specialised

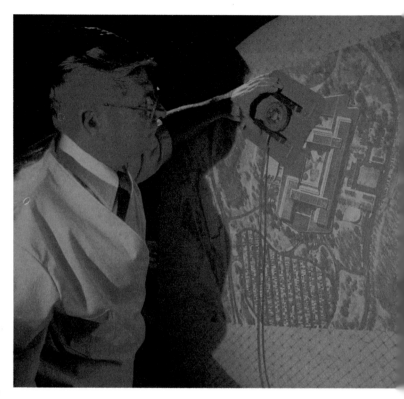

Above: Large-scale aerial images gathered by high-tech cameras are still crucially important to the world's intelligence services. Here, a CIA analyst examines one such reconnaissance photo.

Below: This dramatic, if somewhat poor quality, view of three Libyan Ilyushin IL-76 transport aircraft serves to demonstrate the visual capabilities of the AN/AVQ-26 Pave Tack targeting system.

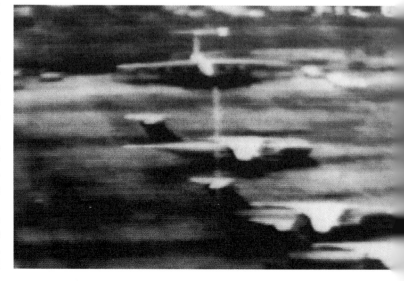

Above: A photographic image from an airborne oblique camera shows part of the city of Los Angeles. At this range, area coverage is wide, and detail is general.

Above: A 4x magnification of the first image (left) begins to reveal more visual detail of the area under scrutiny. Image clarity remains high despite the enlargement.

Above: A 16x enlargement of the first image greatly increases the visual detail available for further analysis by the experts. Analysts will pore over such shots for hours.

Above: Pushing the boundaries of visual clarity to the limits, this 48x magnification nevertheless reveals individual car models and lettering on building signs.

films, for example high-resolution colour reversal stock, or the false-colour film used to detect camouflage. Choice of film must be a matter of compromise: use a high-resolution film, and the exposure time will have risen, increasing the effects of image motion.

On a dedicated photo-reconnaissance aircraft, cameras are carried in one or more custom-designed internal bays. A look at several aircraft types will give the general idea.

Typical installations

The lower part of the RF-4C nose, including the chin fairing, houses optical cameras located on three stations. From the front aft, these are usually one KS-72 or KS-87 forward facing cameras, one KA-56A low-altitude camera, and one KA-55A high-altitude panoramic camera.

On the Mirage F1CR-200, two patterns of optical camera may be carried within the nose-mounted blister fairing. Intended for medium/low level use, the Omera 40 is fitted with a 3in (75mm) lens, while the longer focal length Omera 35 is used for vertical coverage during high-altitude missions.

For strategic reconnaissance at very high altitudes, much longer focal lengths are needed. On the SR-71, long focal-length cameras could be carried in the chine stations, a panoramic camera in the interchangeable nose. SR-71 imagery declassified for general release (such as photos of the results of the US Libyan raid) were usually taken by vertical cameras, probably of 24in (60cm) focal length.

The oblique view

A key element of the tactical flexibility offered by the RF-5E is the use of pallet-mounted sensors which can easily be changed as required for the individual mission. One permanent part of the aircraft's sensor fit was a single KS-87D1 camera mounted behind a sloped window in the extreme nose of the aircraft. This could be fitted with a 6in (15cm) or 12in (30cm) lens.

Most of the sensors are mounted on interchangeable pallets, four patterns of which were proposed. Pallet 1 was designed for low- and medium-altitude missions, and contained a KA-56E and KA-95B panoramic camera with lenses of 3in (7.5cm) and 12in (30cm) focal length respectively.

Pallet 2 was optimised for high-altitude, panoramic, or medium-range standoff photography, and was based around a KA-93B6 panoramic camera fitted with a 24in (60cm) lens. From an altitude of between 10,000 and 50,000ft (3,048 and 15,240m), this unit would provide cross-track coverage of up to 41 miles (66km) when used at a scan angle of 145°. The resolution on the resulting 61×4.5in (155×11cm) negative would be good enough to allow individual vehicles to be clearly shown in photos taken from 40,000ft (12,192m). A second camera on the pallet, a 3in (7.5cm) KA-56E, could be used during low-altitude sorties.

Attempting to overfly a target area can produce problems. In peacetime, it is rarely practical, while the modern SAM and snap up/down air-to-air missile make overflights hazardous in time of war. One solution is to use an oblique camera for standoff photography, a technique often referred to as LOROP (Long-Range Oblique Photography).

This was the intended role of Pallet 3, whose KS-147A camera had a massive lens of 66in (167cm) focal length. This could be set to take a series of four, three, or two overlapping photos at changing depression angles in order to cover a ground swarth, or a series of photos all taken at the same fixed depression angle to create a strip map presentation.

The SR-71 could carry LOROP cameras of 60in (152cm) focal length or more. These give a resolution of down to 30in (76cm) at 60 miles (96km) slant range, allowing the aircraft to avoid overflying hostile territory on some missions.

Israel's F-4E(S) is equipped with the General Dynamics HIAC camera of 66in (168cm) focal length, operating through side and bottom-mounted oblique windows in the aircraft nose. This version was supplied under a programme designated Peace Jack. Even this is far from being the ultimate LOROP camera. Itek's PC/ES-183C has a focal length of 72in (182.7cm), and it is likely that even longer focal lengths are fitted to classified systems. Developed by Eastman Kodak and Recon/Optical, the CA-990 camera is able to stand off up to 200nm (370km) from a target. The body of the camera is more than 11ft (3.35m) long, and houses a 110in (280cm) lens. Tests carried out in 1989 on behalf of an unidentified foreign customer showed a theoretical resolution of 1ft (30cm) at a range of 114 miles (183km).

Oblique cameras can also be pod-mounted. One example is Itek's 66in (168cm) focal length KA-102, while the same company's ES-183C mentioned earlier can be supplied in a pod, or in a conformal version for installation under the belly of an F-16. For the Mirage series, Dassault and Omera have developed the Harold pod, a 1,500lb (680kg) unit designed for long-range oblique photography, which is fitted with an Omera 38 camera mounting a 67in (170cm) focal-length lens. The massive CA-990 camera described in the previous paragraph can also be carried externally under an F-15 or F-4 in a housing based on a 600 US gal (2,271 litre) centreline tank.

The Dassault/Omera COR2 pod is lighter than the Harold pod, weighing only 880lb (400kg). Given this weight, it has

Above left: Mounted on the underside of a Danish Saab Draken, the Swedish FFV Red Baron recce pod houses an IRLS and a variety of support systems.

Above: This view of an RAF airfield taken with an IRLS reveals various "hot-spots" in white. Note the shade of the ground immediately behind aircraft running their engines.

no LOROP camera, so must rely on more conventional designs such as the Omera 35 vertical camera or the Omera 70 panoramic camera. It also carries a Super Cyclope IR linescanner.

IR works by night

As their name suggests, IR linescanners observe a narrow strip of terrain on either side of and below the aircraft at infra-red wavelengths, relying on the aircraft's forward motion to gradually build up an image of the terrain being overflown. If a conventional camera is to be used at night, the aircraft must release photo-flares able to illuminate the target area. An IR scanner relies on heat radiated by the target, so works equally well by night as by day.

Equipments of this type are widely used for night reconnaissance. Perhaps the best-known early examples were the EMI system including the recce pod carried by Royal Air Force Jaguars and F-4 Phantoms, and the FFV Red Baron pod. In the UK, IR linescan technology is now a specialisation of British Aerospace. In 1987 the company signed a deal with Fairchild Weston which covered manufacture of the latest IRLS 4000 system in the USA.

Many aircraft carry internally mounted IR scanners. For example, the third location on RF-5E Pallet 1 was occupied by an RS-710E infra-red scanner operating in the 8-14 micron

Above: Its performance may not be that special, but its intelligence-gathering abilities and versatility have made the Grumman OV-1D Mohawk a popular and effective *aircraft. Clearly visible is the very prominent fuselage-mounted pod, this being used to house an APS-94 SLAR. The aircraft can also carry a variety of cameras and receivers.*

band. When the Mirage F1CR-200 entered service with ER/2/33 Savoie in September 1983, the aircraft's IR sensor was not yet ready for service. Located in the lower edge of the starboard intake in place of the cannon carried in this location by the fighter version, this is an SAT SCM Super Cyclope linescan unit. Data from Super Cyclope is transmitted via a datalink to the SARA ground station.

In an effort to extend RF-4B service life by a further eight years, a batch of 30 were reworked in 1978 under the Sensor Update and Refurbishment Effort (SURE). Equipment added included the AAD-5 infra-red reconnaissance set, and the APD-10 sideways-looking airborne radar (SLAR).

Sideways looking radar

Since the 1950s, this latter type of equipment has been used for all-weather reconnaissance. On the RF-4C for example, the aircraft's AAS-118 infra-red detecting set was backed up by a Goodyear APQ-102A sideways looking radar. This recorded on photographic film a radar image of a broad strip of terrain on either side of the flight path.

Recce Phantoms such as the RF-4B, -4C and -4E have been updated to match modern requirements. The original APQ-102A radar was initially replaced by the Goodyear UPD-4 synthetic-aperture sideways looking radar. The twin antennas are gimbal-mounted, and may be moved automatically in flight to maintain a constant look angle. The system can be set to a number of operating modes, recording fixed-target imagery only or mixed and moving target data.

Luftwaffe RF-4Es have been retrofitted with the newer Goodyear UPD-6 radar. This incorporates a data link which is used to transmit real-time radar data back to ground stations, a feature also incorporated in an extended-range version of the UPD-4. In a similar move, the USAF has updated its RF-4Cs with Goodyear's UPD-8, which uses a wideband datalink to pass information to the ground. The latest Goodyear SLAR is the UPD-9, a pod-mounted system which can be carried under an F-18. Based on the earlier -4, it too has a data link, but lacks the long range of the -8.

The TR-1A carries a Hughes Advanced Synthetic-Aperture Radar System (ASARS), as did some SR-71s. Previous SLARs looked out at 90° to the aircraft flight path, but this new system can be pointed at any angle. According to the manufacturer, ASARS-2 is a "multi-generation leap" in SLAR technology. Maximum range is around 100 miles (160km) when the aircraft is flying at 75,000ft (22,860m). By adding the latest VHSIC (Very High Speed Integrated Circuit) electronics to the current ASARS-2 version, Hughes has also created a pod-mounted variant.

The French Air Force prefers to package its SLAR in a pod, so has ordered the Thomson-CSF Raphael TH all-weather reconnaissance system for its Mirage F1CR force. From an aircraft flying at around 25,000ft (7,620m), this I/J-band radar can observe a swarth of terrain 25 miles (40km) wide from a stand-off range of 37 miles (60km), passing imagery to the ground via a datalink. Under these conditions, resolution is around 10ft (3m).

Pictures via radio

Datalinks solve one of the oldest problems in tactical reconnaissance, that of getting imagery into the hands of ground commanders while it is still fresh. Front-line combat units need to receive the current tactical position, not a record of where the enemy was several hours ago or more. The RF-4C tries to solve this problem by processing the film while the aircraft is in flight, and if necessary ejecting the resulting photographs in a cartridge which could be picked up by front-line personnel.

If a conventional camera installation is used, the film must be removed from the cameras once the aircraft has landed, then rushed to the processing laboratory. The latter facility needs chemicals, large amounts of pure water (a commodity sometimes in short supply at a field location), plus time — between one and three hours. Only then is imagery available for analysis.

The EO revolution

Where images of the highest quality are required, the traditional camera and film remain the best solution, but a new generation of sensor systems trades resolution for real-time data. Replace the photographic film with an imaging array based on charge-coupled device (CCD) technology, and the image can be obtained in digital form. Such a signal can be recorded on magnetic tape, or transmitted by downlink in much the same way as is done in some IR linescanner systems.

Given ideal lighting and visibility conditions, a photographic film can resolve up to 200 lines in a millimetre of emulsion. The best available from a CCD EO system is around 50. In practice, environmental factors such as atmospheric haze and aircraft vibration will often reduce the performance of film-based cameras to a level closer to that of the EO system, so the trade-off is not as severe as it might seem at first sight.

The main problem in sending video images over a datalink is the sheer amount of information which even a low resolution image can contain. Transmission of a single monochrome image from a 592 × 440 pixel monitor can involve between 150 and 680 kilobytes of data. Using a datalink able to handle 9,600 bits per second — the best possible from a landline — transmission of this single image will take around two minutes, while a good UHF or VHF radio link might do the job in one minute.

A partial solution exists in the form of algorithms which compress the data by a factor of ten or more, but the effect of these is partially offset by the need to use an error-correction algorithm able to overcome the effects of electronic noise on the link. In practice, imagery can be under the scrutiny of an analyst within a minute or so of the picture being taken.

This development will revolutionise tactical reconnaissance operations. Maximum range of a datalinked recce system can be of the order of 250 miles (400km), or up to 560 miles (900km) if an airborne relay aircraft is used. After making a run over the target area, aircraft will be able to fly out of the threat zone, back towards or into friendly airspace if necessary, make datalink contact with a ground station, then download the images which it has gathered. Before making contact with the ground station, the systems operator on a two-seat aircraft would have been able to review the information on his cockpit displays, selecting the best and most relevant for transmission.

Equally important is the fact that the aircraft will be freed from the time-consuming chore of returning to base after observing each new set of targets. A typical low-altitude photo

Below: The specialised nose bay built into the RF-4C Phantom II can house three cameras, these usually consisting of one forward oblique, one 180° panoramic and one low-altitude unit.

Right: Once back from a mission, the recce "take" is removed from the RF-4C, quickly processed, and passed onto the operating unit's analysts for interpretation, as shown here.

mission might involve a two-hour sortie against a target 500 miles (800km) from base. The sole productive part of this mission might be the 50 mile (80km) run in to the target, followed by the run out. The rest of the mission is spent getting to the general operating area, then returning to base. A further unproductive period will be spent while the ground crew remove the film and other records, load fresh media and refuel the aircraft. The retrofitted RF-4C would be able to withdraw to a safe distance, rendezvous with a tanker, then return to the battle zone.

The SR-71 was probably the first aircraft to fly with EO cameras coupled to datalinks. In the late 1980s, the USAF planned to provide its RF-4C fleet with a similar capability, but this project was abandoned as being uneconomic given the age of the airframes.

The proposed modification was part of a larger programme known as the Advanced Tactical Air Reconnaissance System (ATARS). This is intended to develop modular EO and IR sensors, plus datalinks, suitable for use in USAF, USN and USMC aircraft and RPVs. Three main sensor types are planned. The daylight sensors are a low-altitude wide field-of-view unit, and a medium-altitude system for stand-off missions. A third will be used by night. The ATARS project is also investigating the potential usefulness of recce sensors operating in at near-IR wavelengths traditionally associated with low-light TV systems. The likely cost of the entire programme has been estimated at up to $5 billion over the next two decades.

On the ground, the signal from an ATARS-equipped aircraft would be handled by the Joint Service Imagery Processing System (JSIPS). Based on ruggedised VAX and mini-VAX computers, and housed in six transportable shelters, JSIPS would be able to take the downlinked data, process it, and merge it with information from other intelligence sources, then transmit the results to the end users.

Left: A rare glimpse inside one of the camera bays on board an OV-1 Mohawk reveals a KS-61 panoramic camera. Clearly visible within the hinged access cover is the built-in glazed panel for viewing.

Above: The dramatic launch of an Israeli-built Mazlat Pioneer RPV from a US Navy ship. Equipment for its mission is housed within the fuselage body, with a transparent bottom viewing panel an option.

The predicted future decline in the US defence budget had made the development of a dedicated "RF" replacement for the USAF's elderly RF-4C fleet unlikely, even before the political changes which swept Eastern Europe in late 1989. As a result, the Follow-On Tactical Reconnaissance System which replaces the -4C is likely to be F-15 or F-16 carrying the ATARS sensors in a pod.

Cameras can also be supplied with facilities to accept film or EO sensing elements, while existing cameras such as the CAI KS-153 used on USMC RF-4s can be converted to EO operation. Another obvious application for EO cameras is aboard remotely piloted vehicles (RPVs). Teledyne Ryan Model 324 Scarab RPVs purchased by Egypt in the late 1980s have been used to carry KS-153 EO cameras with 24in (61cm) lenses. Unlike film cameras, which use forward-motion compensation (FMC) to counteract image motion, the KS-153 is able to achieve the same effect using microprocessor technology.

Europe is also moving from conventional film-based cameras to digital systems which can download information via datalink. West Germany and the Netherlands both have requirements for an ATARS-type system. In 1987 the US and the Netherlands announced a project to develop an ATARS-compatible EO pod for the F-16, while pod-mounted payloads suitable for the Mirage F1 include the Thomson-CSF TMV 018 optronic pod for real-time reconnaissance. The French company TRT is developing the TEORS electro-optical camera, a unit based on CCD technology.

Scout helicopters can also be fitted out with TV sensors and datalinks, and used for tactical reconnaissance. During Exercise Reforger in 1988, a modified Bell OH-58D was used to gather high-quality monochrome and colour tactical imagery, transmitting this back to brigade, division and corps commanders within minutes. Experience showed that data could be received when the aircraft was up to 26 miles (42km) away, flying at heights as low as 100ft (30m). If a link could not be established, the aircraft could record up to 50 images, before popping up to a higher altitude in order to transmit them.

The commercial availability of cameras which use magnetic disks rather than film as a recording medium is useful to the intelligence community. During trials carried out in 1989, the crew of a US Navy P-3 Orion operating over the Gulf of Mexico used a Canon camera fitted with a zoom lens to take colour imagery of a Soviet intelligence-gathering vessel. The 2in (5cm) magnetic disk was removed from the camera, and its data transmitted via a satellite communications link, giving analysts based near the Patuxent River Naval Air Test Center in Maryland near-real-time intelligence imagery.

Cameras, SLAR systems and EO sensors are all designed to detect the physical presence of threat systems. In parallel with such systems, air forces also deploy aircraft equipped for electronic intelligence gathering. The art is generally referred to as "sigint" (signals intelligence); the more widely used term "elint" (electronic intelligence) is strictly speaking the gathering of signals from targets such as radars. Interception of communications is known as "comint" whereas

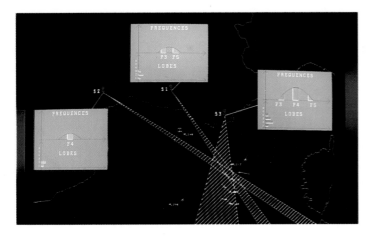

Above: By using triangulation. the position of hostile emitters can be established. While in the range of such emitters, recce aircraft must try to avoid giving their position away if the mission is to succeed.

Below: An autopilot controls the Pioneer RPV from take-off until it lands. Here. one of the RPVs snags in the vertically strung retrieval net at the end of a sortie. Mission endurance is 6-9 hours.

"radint" tries to utilise stray emissions such as interference from the ignition systems of internal combustion engines.

Signals intelligence

Sigint operations are intended to identify threat systems. Signals detected are analysed, and the results compared with the data held in a threat data base so that the identity of the emitter can be deduced.

Each type of radar has its own electronic characteristics. Once identified and recorded, these are known as the emitter's "signature". This data is used to build up a database of all the emitters deployed by the target nation. Once this has been done, each pattern of emitter can be reliably identified whenever it is encountered in the future, helping intelligence staff to monitor the deployment of the target nation's forces, compiling what is termed the "electronic order of battle".

Elint also provides useful short-term tactical information. By comparing all detected signals against known radar signatures, it is possible to identify the radar from which it came. Data gathered during elint operations can then be used to programme the threat libraries of Electronic Support Measure (ESM) equipment. ESM plays a major role in maritime-patrol missions. If covert coverage is needed it could well be the primary sensor. Even if radar and other sensors can be used, ESM still plays a major role. For a start, it can detect targets which may still be beyond radar range. It can also be correlated with the output from other sensors, being used to help identify radar targets, for example.

The exact mix of signatures emitted by a distant warship or aircraft will often allow the platform to be identified. If several ships or aircraft in a formation operate similar radars. these sets must be tuned to slightly different frequencies so that one does not interfere with another. Careful measurement of radar frequency can thus provide an indication of how many ships or aircraft are present.

Use of the expression "target nation" rather than "enemy" several paragraphs ago was deliberate. Sigint is one form of intelligence gathering which is widely practised in peacetime. Most nations spy on their neighbours by means of sigint, with neutrals or even one's allies not necessarily excluded from the target list. The unique quality of elint as a reconnaissance tool is that it may be continuously used from peacetime, through times of tension and crisis, and during war, thus building up a long-term picture denied to other types of sensor.

Aircraft tasked with sigint carry radio receivers, signal processors, displays and recorders able to detect the presence and bearing of radiated signals. Some degree of analysis and classification may well be attempted, but the main task is to record these signals for later study by ground-based analysts.

Receivers can be of the crystal-video and IFM type, a solution widely adopted on present-day aircraft, or more advanced wide-band designs using SAW technology. The move to more sophisticated receivers is a result of the growing complexity of radio and radar emissions. The equipment not only deals with high signal densities, but also with techniques such as frequency diversity, frequency agility, PRF stagger and jitter. The use of software-controlled radar systems allows the easy introduction of new radar modes. These greatly complicate the analyst's task, making new emitters difficult to identify.

In the absence of a dedicated elint aircraft, most users will have to make do with alternative sensors. One possible approach is to equip a normal fighter with an internally mounted sigint system or an add-on sigint pod. Probably the best-known tactical electronic reconnaissance system of this type is the Litton Amecom ALQ-125 Tactical Electronic Reconnaissance (TEREC) system.

To help with the anti-radar battle, the USAF retrofitted a portion of its RF-4C fleet with this equipment, plus the Ford Aerospace AVQ-26 Pave Tack laser designator/fire-control system. An initial batch of 18 was initially reworked, but smaller numbers have subsequently been modified.

The TEREC system monitors hostile radar signals, analysing these, then identifying the emitters involved and deducing their position. This electronic order of battle (EOB) information is displayed in the rear cockpit. This is just the information which will be needed by the other members of the USAF anti-radar team — the F-4G and the EF-111. Having identified the radars and radio transmitters which represent the greatest threat, the TEREC Phantoms use their Pave Tack EO systems to mark these for attack by strike aircraft.

At one time it was planned that the aircraft would carry a pod-mounted digital datalink, allowing the EOB informa-

Above: Dripping antennae from a host of underfuselage points, and with slab-sided SLAR pods and a mission nose, this Lockheed TR-1 is well and truly geared for one of its high-altitude tactical recce flights.

Below Though primarily used in the ECCM training role, the bulbous-nosed Canberra T.17 could easily be put to good use in the ECM/ ESM role in wartime. The distinctive blisters house active jamming units.

tion to be relayed in real-time to other users. Although flight-tested on the RF-4C/TEREC trials aircraft, this was not adopted for service.

TEREC has proved successful, but is now rather dated. For example, it can only observe a relatively small number of emitters per second. A more modern system is the Thomson-CSF Syrel, a podded sensor which relies on ground processing. The pod is 11ft (3.57m) long, 16.5in (42cm) in diameter, and weighs 584lb (265kg). It consists of an antenna array, superhet receiver, a processor (controlled by a programme loaded before flight, plus a control box), a magnetic recorder

Above: Several nations continue to make good use of the RF-4 Phantom II to meet their reconnaissance needs. Though primarily used for the gathering of photographic data, the RF-4 can also carry an APQ-102 SLAR in the fuselage, along with an AAS-18A IRLS. THe nose radome houses an APQ-99 forward-looking radar, and two photoflash packs are mounted just ahead of the fin.

and data link. It can be carried on a small fighter such as the Mirage 2000. The pod covers the C to J bands, and has a high enough sensitivity to intercept radar signals via their back lobes. Selectivity is high enough to allow emitter discrimination in a signal-dense environment.

The Syrel ground station is housed in a 3.5 ton (3.6 tonne) cabin 12.7ft (3.88m) long, 8ft (2.44m) wide and 7.7ft (2.33m) high. Data obtained either via the data link or from a tape cassette recorded by the pod is processed by computer and displayed on two operator consoles.

Killing the radar

ASTAR is a more modern system from the same company. Formerly known as STAR, this has been ordered to equip French Air Force Mirage F1CR aircraft. By early 1988 this had been tested in prototype form, undergoing trials which included flights close to the East German border. Controlled by a reprogrammable management unit incorporating four microprocessors, ASTAR is designed to process data from up to 20 emitters per second.

Like Syrel, the system incorporates a data link able to send information to a ground-based processing centre. The design of this was still at the proposal stage in early 1988, but was expected to include powerful computing and display facilities.

The F1CR is a single seater, but, with an eye to the export market, Thomson-CSF drew up plans for a operator's display

suitable for two-seat aircraft. This incorporates a circular PPI CRT, a smaller rectangular screen for tabular data, plus a simple keyboard. A smaller circular CRT in the front cockpit would repeat the PPI information. This late-1980s initiative paid off when the system was selected as part of Japan's programme to convert some F-4EJ Phantoms to the recce role.

Twenty-five years ago, few air arms paid much attention to anti-radar technology of any kind. Today, any nation which faces a sophisticated anti-aircraft threat must invest heavily in EW equipment such as radar-warning receivers, chaff-dispensers and jammers. Although valuable, these remain essentially passive, and much less attention is being given to active, or ''hard-kill'' solutions.

Although some custom-modified anti-radar aircraft were used during the final stages of World War II, then again during the Korean War, the concept lay dormant until the Vietnam War. Faced with the threat posed by Soviet-supplied SA-2 Guideline SAMs, the USAF modified some two-seat F-100F Super Sabres, installing equipment designed to detect and locate hostile radars. The programme was codenamed ''Wild Weasel'', and this designation has been applied to the follow-on F-105G, the EF-4C, and the current F-4G.

Radar-hunting is a specialised skill. Pilots assigned to F-4G units must have a minimum of 500 hours in tactical fighters. The electronic warfare officers in the original F-100F Weasels used in Vietnam were B-52 or RC-135 operators pressed into service in the new role. Today's back-seaters are hand-picked graduates from a 25-week training course at the USAF's EWO school at Mather AFB.

Trainees learn to cope with the complexity of the APR-38 during medium-level missions, then move to treetop height to practise more realistically. Then its back to medium altitude for weapons training, returning to low level to put the new skills into practice.

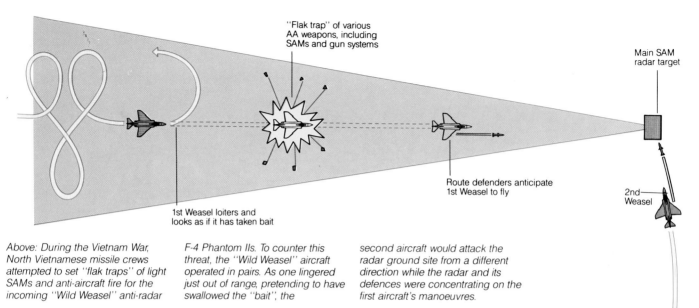

"Flak trap" of various AA weapons, including SAMs and gun systems

Main SAM radar target

Route defenders anticipate 1st Weasel to fly

2nd Weasel

1st Weasel loiters and looks as if it has taken bait

Above: During the Vietnam War, North Vietnamese missile crews attempted to set "flak traps" of light SAMs and anti-aircraft fire for the incoming "Wild Weasel" anti-radar

F-4 Phantom IIs. To counter this threat, the "Wild Weasel" aircraft operated in pairs. As one lingered just out of range, pretending to have swallowed the "bait", the

second aircraft would attack the radar ground site from a different direction while the radar and its defences were concentrating on the first aircraft's manoeuvres.

Tactics for F-4G operations have been devised by the 562nd TFTS. Part of the 37th TFW and based at George AFB, California — within easy flying distance of the Red Flag tactical range at Tonopah in Nevada — this unit "wrote the book" on F-4G operations. Instructor Pilots and EWOs can use the "friendly enemy" facilities at Tonopah to test their tactics against the latest simulated (and in some cases real) electronic threats.

Two simulators at George AFB help prepare crews for the task of flying anti-radar missions. All-round visual displays create an external "view" while a complete functioning APR-38 allows trainee EWOs to operate the system, freezing or re-running tactical situations as required in training. Trainer sessions also teach EWOs how to recognise and cope with APR-38 failures.

The F-4G Weasels were initially deployed alongside standard F-4Es. These operated as hunter/killer formations in which the F-4Es "rode shotgun" for the Weasel, relying on the APR-38-equipped F-4G to direct them to targets. This simple move greatly expanded the usefulness of the numerically small F-4G force.

At first, the basic formation was reported to have been a three aircraft flight, but a more flexible philosophy was later evolved in which F-4Gs and -4Es were mixed as required. Basic formation became one F-4G plus one F-4E, with further E models being used as required to provide extra firepower.

1987 saw the West German-based 52nd TFW — European operators of the F-4G — phase in the F-16 as a replacement for the F-4Es. These aircraft could be fitted with the older

AGM-45 Shrike anti-radiation missile (ARM), but the latest F-16 Block 40/42 have the digital electronics needed to operate the more effective AGM-88 high-speed anti-radiation missile (HARM).

The primary target of the Wild Weasels in Vietnam was SAM sites, but the current philosophy assigns highest priority to mobile early warning and acquisition radars. Target selection must be tackled with care, with the scarce Weasels being assigned to "take out" mobile targets. Radars and other emitters at fixed sites can be attacked with conventional strike formations, but successful attacks against transportable and mobile systems require the unique target-location capabilities of the APR-38.

The task in hand is "defence suppression". Ideally, that is done by knocking out the radar, but forcing a temporary shutdown may be enough to get the mission done. In some cases, the hostile radars may remain active, but still be effectively countered. Radars and operators tied up in the task of trying to launch at a Weasel without becoming its victim may fail to spot a low-flying strike force. Even if they do, they cannot give the attackers all their attention. Ignoring the Weasels would be tantamount to suicide.

Since the Vietnam War, the quality and reaction time of Soviet-style defence radars has markedly improved. For much of the time, the Weasels will probably stay low, with individual aircraft popping up to examine the enemy signals. Trainee crews at George AFB in the early 1980s flew up to 30 sorties in order to practise the skills of flying at heights of 250ft (75m) or less. Western Europe's relatively flat terrain forces Weasel crews to be ingenious in their use of the minimal

Above: Northrop's AGM-136A Tacit Rainbow anti-radar drone, seen here on an A-6E Intruder, can fly for over 80 minutes, and loiter while waiting to identify a target.

Below: The USAF's current "Wild Weasel" team consists of the F-16C and the F-4G, the former acting as "bomb truck" for the latter on their hazardous missions.

terrain cover available. The shallowest valleys, and even the tree line must be exploited. Indiscriminate use cannot be made of the ECM pod; early operating experience showed that the ALQ-119 can interfere with the APR-38.

It takes a special kind of aircrewman to fly and operate the Weasel. Victor Belenko, the Soviet pilot who flew his MiG-25 Foxbat to Japan in 1976, explained to his biographer John Barron how lecturers at the Soviet Air Force's Armavir training centre claimed that Weasel crews were either highly paid mercenaries, or flew under the influence of drugs.

In practice, F-4G crews are closer to the world of the movie *Star Wars* than to that of hypothetical drug-crazed mercenaries. In 1982, the British aviation magazine *Air In-ternational* asked 562nd TFTS Bear instructor Lt-Col. Sam Peacock how big a part intuition played in his job. "When you know what this gear can do, and how what's actually happening [in an attack] may be different, its almost as if 'The Force is with you'," explained Peacock. Like *Star Wars* hero Luke Skywalker, the F-4G crews develop the skills to react faster than their craft's automatic systems. "A slightly different tone will let you know [the attack] is not right, and you can pull off three or four seconds before the computer gives you the information on the CRT screen."

West Germany plans to deploy the anti-radar Tornado ECR, and the Soviet Air Force has fielded the specialised MiG-25 Foxbat F, but no other nations have adopted the Wild Weasel philosophy. The high unit cost of these specialised aircraft, the need for regular updating of the on-board systems, and unwillingness to divert part of an air arm's fighter strength to a specialised role are all factors against the deployment of specialised anti-radar strike aircraft.

Some companies have suggested the use of pod-mounted "Weasel" systems which could allow a standard fighter-bomber to fly anti-radar missions. For example, an optional localisation processor can be fitted to the mid-section of the Thomson-CSF ASTAR elint pod to allow the aircraft to fly Wild Weasel-type operations.

Even the USAF is now having second thoughts about its plans to develop a replacement aircraft for the F-4G. As the number of aircraft able to carry ARMs such as AGM-88 grows, and the future of the Northrop AGM-136A Tacit Rainbow anti-radiation drone looks more secure, some argue that a combination of these two weapons will cope with the anti-radar mission. The UK and France seem to agree, placing their faith in a new generation of lightweight ARMs which can be carried as a supplement to (rather than as a replacement for) normal ordnance, giving all fighter-bombers a potential anti-radar capability.

Dassault-Breguet Mirage F1CR-200

Developed to replace the delta-winged Mirage IIIR and IIIRD, the recce version of the F.1 is based on the F1C-200 variant, which features a 3in (8cm) stretch of the forward fuselage, and a fixed in-flight refuelling probe mounted slightly off-set to starboard just ahead of the windscreen.

Two F1CR-200 prototypes were built, the first making its maiden flight on 20 November 1981. First production example was completed in November 1982 and the type entered service in September 1983 with the commissioning of ER 2/33 Savoie.

Most obvious external features of the CR-200 are the in-flight refuelling boom, and the blister fairing beneath the nose for the aircraft's sensors. Two patterns of optical camera may be carried within the nose-mounted blister fairing. Intended for medium/low level use, the Omera 40 is fitted with a 75mm lens, while the longer focal length Omera 35 is used for vertical coverage during high altitude missions.

When the ER 2/33 commissioned, the aircraft's IR sensor was not yet ready for service. Located in the lower edge of

Left: The Mirage F1CR carries its cameras and IR linescanner internally, but radar and elint recce missions require the use of an external pod such as the ASTAC elint system or Raphael TH SLAR.

the starboard intake in place of the cannon carried in this location by the fighter version, this is a SAT SCM Super Cyclope linescan unit. Data from Super Cyclope is transmitted via a data link to the SARA (Système Aero-Transportable de Reconnaissance Aerienne) ground station. Made up of eight caravans, this provides airmobile facilities for image processing and interpretation. It also has datalink equipment able to receive real-time signals from the Super Cyclope IR scanner.

Changes were also made to the avionics to match the aircraft to its new role. A Thomson-CSF Cyrano IVMR radar is installed instead of the normal Cyrano IV, and this offers additional operating modes for ground-mapping, contour-mapping, air-to-ground ranging and blind let-down. A Sagem Uliss 47 inertial platform is linked to an ESD 182 navigation computer.

The Mirage F1 can also be used in the anti-radar role, carrying either the Thomson-CSF ASTAC elint pod to detect hostile emitters, or the Matra Armat anti-radar missile. Another payload is the 1,245lb (565kg) Thomson-CSF Raphael TH sideways-looking radar pod. Also known as TVM 064, this entered service at the end of 1985.

F1CRs have been used in support of French combat operations in Chad. At least one mission was flown against the Libyan-held air base of Ouadi Doum in January 1987 prior to a strike mission against the airfield by Jaguars.

No export customers have ordered dedicated recce F1s, but some use centreline reconnaissance pods. Iraq operates the Harold camera pod on its Mirage F1EQ-4s, for example, while Quatari F1DEs can carry the COR2 camera pod, and Moroccan F1EH aircraft use a similar pod developed under a Franco-Moroccan programme.

Right: The desert camouflage scheme and refuelling probe on this F1CR are reminders of France's continued military involvement in the defence of its former colonies in Africa, particularly Chad.

Role: Reconnaissance fighter.
Length: 50ft 2.5in (15.3m).
Height: 14ft 9in (4.5m).
Wingspan: 27ft 6.75in (8.40m).
Weights — empty: 16,310lb (7,400kg).
  Loaded: 24,030lb (16,200kg).
  Max. takeoff: 35,715lb (16,200kg).
Powerplant: One Snecma Atar 9K-50.
Rating: 15,873lb (7,200kg) in full afterburner.
Tactical radius: 230-750nm (420-1,390km) hi-lo-hi.
Max. speed: Mach 2.2.
Ceiling: 65,600ft (20,000m).
Armament: Magic air-to-air missiles+two 30mm cannon.

Lockheed F-117A "Senior Trend"

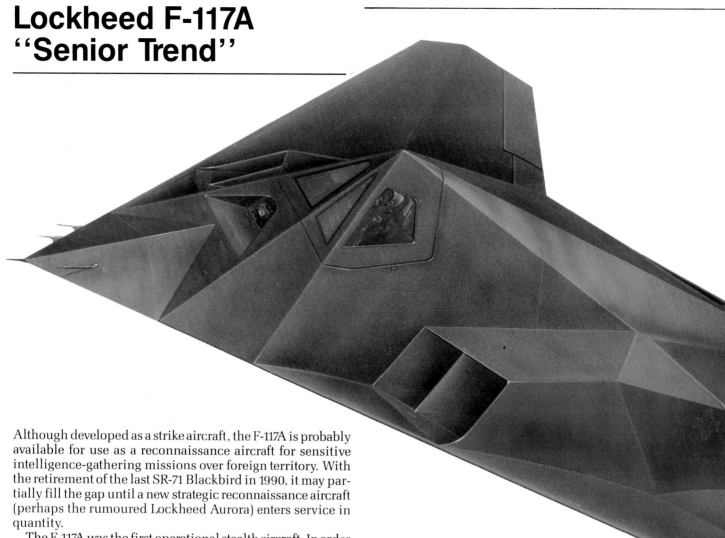

Although developed as a strike aircraft, the F-117A is probably available for use as a reconnaissance aircraft for sensitive intelligence-gathering missions over foreign territory. With the retirement of the last SR-71 Blackbird in 1990, it may partially fill the gap until a new strategic reconnaissance aircraft (perhaps the rumoured Lockheed Aurora) enters service in quantity.

The F-117A was the first operational stealth aircraft. In order to prove the technology needed for a fighter of negligible radar cross-section, two XST prototypes were built under the Defense Advanced Research Projects Agency's "Have Blue" programme. These were about two-thirds the size of today's F-117A. The first flew in January 1978, the second the following spring. Both were destined to crash. The first was lost in May 1978, but the prototype survived until May 1980, providing the experience needed to create the full-size aircraft.

Full-scale development of the F-117A fighter was ordered by the USAF in 1978 under the codename "Senior Trend". The first flight was in June 1981, and the aircraft entered operational service in October 1983. Delivery of a fleet of 59 was completed in 1990.

Two techniques are used to minimise radar cross-section.

By building up the fuselage from a series of flat facets, and by using only three highly swept angles in the wing planform, the designers ensured that much of the radar energy striking the aircraft would be deflected at harmless angles, rather than being reflected directly back toward the enemy radar. Radar reflectivity was further minimised by covering the airframe with sheets of radar-absorbent material (RAM).

The inlets which supply air to the aircraft's twin F404 engines are thought to incorporate a screen intended to prevent the ingress and subsequent reflection of radar energy, a technique first tested on Firebee reconnaissance drones dur-

Right: The first photo ever released of the F-117A seems to have been deliberately chosen to conceal rather than reveal the aircraft's true shape. The wing is more highly swept and the aircraft less hump-backed than the photo suggests.

Left: At the time this drawing was prepared, no good photos of the F-117A inlet were available, so the artist was not able to show the vertical grill structure which admits air into the engines, but makes the inlet virtually invisible to long-range search radars.

Role: Reconnaissance/strike fighter.
Length: 65.92ft (20.09m).
Wingspan: 43.3ft (13.21m).
Weights — empty: ?
  Max. takeoff: 52,507lb (23,813kg).
Powerplant(s): Two non-afterburning General Electric F404 turbofans.
Rating: 10,800-12,500lb (4,900-5,670kg).
Tactical radius: 800-1,200nm (1,500-2,200km).
Max. speed: High subsonic.
Armament: c.4,000lb (1,800kg) of stores carried internally.

ing the Vietnam War. These experiments used a fine wire mesh, but the screen in the F-117A inlet is thought to be made up from a knife-edged grill structure. The exhaust from the engines is ejected from wide slot-shaped outlets in the rear fuselage. These mask the engines from radar, and shape the efflux into wide plumes which quickly cool, reducing the aircraft's IR signature.

No radar is carried, so that the aircraft's location is not compromised by detectable emissions. A hemispherical housing mounted ahead of the cockpit houses the optics for a combined FLIR and laser-designation system. This may have two fields of view — wide for navigation and target location, and narrow for attack. On recce missions, this sensor could be used to identify and record targets of interest, while the aircraft's weapons bay might be fitted with cameras, IR scanners, or elint receivers.

Given the aircraft's odd shape, it is hardly surprising that it is tricky to fly. Although fitted with an advanced digital fly-by-wire flight control system developed by Lear Siegler, it must still be handled with care, and this has apparently led to its being dubbed the ''Wobbly Goblin''. Three had crashed by the end of the 1980s.

Lockheed SR-71 Blackbird

On 26 April 1962 Lockheed flew the first prototype of design A-12, a Mach 3 aircraft developed for the Central Intelligence Agency as a replacement for the earlier U-2. Deliveries to the CIA started towards the end of the year. Fifteen were built, all but one of which were single seaters.

The experimental YF-12A interceptor variant flown in August 1963 was never adopted for service, but 22 December, 1964 saw the flight of the improved SR-71 Blackbird reconnaissance aircraft.

The first example delivered to the USAF in January 1966 was an SR-71B trainer, but the definitive SR-71A began to replace the A-12 later that year. The A-12 was retired from operational service in 1968, the final sortie ending in tragedy on 5 June when the aircraft and its pilot were lost during an operational mission from Kadena.

A total of 32 SR-71s was built, all but two of which were two-seaters. Aircraft 64-17956 was the first SR-71B trainer, flying for the first time on 2 November 1965. The only other B model was 64-17957. The last SR-71 to be built was 64-17981, the sole example of the SR-71C trainer model. It was created by mating the wings and fuselage of one of the YF-12A interceptors with a forward fuselage originally built as a static test item.

The aircraft entered service with the 4200 Strategic Reconnaissance Wing at Beale AFB, California. Soon afterwards, the unit was reorganised as the 9th Strategic Reconnaissance Wing, operating a mixture of U-2 and SR-71 aircraft.

The aircraft has five equipment bays in the fuselage chines and nose. These carry its highly classified sensor payload. Long focal-length cameras can be carried in the chine stations, panoramic camera in the interchangeable nose. The aircraft can also carry LOROP cameras of 60in (1,524mm) focal length or more. These give a resolution of down to 30in (762mm) at 60 miles (96.5km) slant range, allowing the air-

Role: Strategic reconnaissance aircraft.
Length: 103ft 10in (31.65m).
Height: 18ft 6in (5.64m).
Wingspan: 55ft 7in (16.94).
Weights — empty: 67,500lb (30,618kg).
   Max. takeoff: 172,000lb (78,019kg).
Powerplant(s): Two Pratt & Whitney J58-I turbojets.
Rating: 32,500lb (14,742kg) with A/B.
Max. range: 3,250nm (6,019km).
Max. speed: c. Mach 3.25 at altitude.
Ceiling: c.85,000ft (25,900m).
Armament: None.

Left: Careful rounding of the fuselage and the use of radar-absorbent material in the wing edges allowed Mach 3 performance to be combined with a degree of stealth.

Above: Many SAMs were fired at the SR-71 during a quarter century of operational service, but none scored a hit. The high-flying Blackbird always made it back to base.

craft to avoid overflying hostile territory on some missions.

By the early 1980s, keeping this elderly aircraft operational posed significant problems. The USAF has already replaced some of its older avionic systems, units for which spare parts are now hard to find, while Pratt & Whitney devised schemes to rework engine components.

In the spring of 1988, US Air Force Secretary Edward C. Aldridge revealed that the cost of operating and maintaining the SR-71 fleet was similar to the cost of maintaining two complete wings of tactical fighters. This announcement came shortly after a USAF decision that the number maintained in operational status should be reduced from 12 to six.

Plans to retire the SR-71 were announced in 1989. Suggestions that the Air National Guard take over the Beale-based SR-71 operations were not accepted, and the type was phased out in the spring of 1990.

Three have been passed to NASA's Dryden Flight Research facility, which will use two for high-speed research, and store the third in flyable condition. "At least six" of the remaining 17 have been mothballed, and in theory at least could be reactivated if required.

Below: Almost 30 years after the original A-12 first flew, the SR-71 still looks futuristic, but that sleek exterior concealed equipment and subsystems whose age made spares hard to find, and maintenance very expensive. This eventually forced the type into retirement.

Lockheed U-2R and TR-1

Developed to meet a 1953 USAF/CIA requirement for an air-craft able to operate at extreme altitudes beyond the ceiling of mid-1950s interceptors and SAM systems, Lockheed's U-2 operated with impunity over Soviet territory between July 1956 and April 1960. Designed with an anticipated opera-tional lifetime of only a few years, the aircraft is still in ser-vice, having been returned to production twice — once in the late 1960s to create the U-2R, and again in the late 1970s as the TR-1.

Early production deliveries were made to the CIA, who hired suitable pilots from the USAF to provide them with civilian status. The first mission over Soviet territory was flown on 4 July 1956 by the seventh aircraft to have been built. Some sources credit the U-2 with having flown 20 such mis-sions into Warsaw Pact airspace before a U-2 flown by Francis G. Power's aircraft was downed near Sverdlovsk on 1 May 1960.

The original versions (now all retired from service) were the U-2A; the structurally strengthened and up-engined U-2B; the U-2C with its slightly extended nose, long dorsal equipment fairing, increased fuel capacity, and enlarged in-takes, and the J75-P-13B engine; the U-2D with a modified Q bay able to house specialised sensors or a second crew member; the U-2E with advanced ECM systems; the U-2F with facilities for in-flight refuelling, and the carrier-compatible U-2G and J models. These variants account for a production total of around 55 aircraft (although not all the assigned serials may have been built). All have now been retired.

In 1968 the aircraft was returned to production. The U-2R had first flown in prototype form on 28 August 1967, and had an extended-span wing, longer fuselage, and underwing equipment pods which supplement the volume of the fuselage bays. Twelve were built. The maximum altitude is

Right: In its TR-1 form shown here, Lockheed's high-flying U-2 has outlived its Mach 3 replacement, and is likely to serve well past the year 2000. Its ageing J75 turbojet engine (obtained by cannibalising retired F-105s) will probably be replaced by a modern turbofan such as the F101 or F118, giving a valuable boost to performance.

Role: High-altitude reconnaissance.
Length: 63ft 0in (19.20m).
Height: 16ft 0in (4.88m).
Wingspan: 103ft 0in (31.39m).
Weights — empty: ?
  Max. takeoff: 40,000lb (18,140kg).
Powerplant: One Pratt & Whitney J75-P-13B turbojet.
Rating: 17,000lb (7,710kg) dry thrust.
Max. range: More than 2,600nm (4,800km).
Max. speed: More than 373kts (692km/hr).
Ceiling: 90,000ft (27,400m).
Armament: None.

Below: Posing in front of his TR-1. this pressure-suited pilot is a reminder that the aircraft flies at extreme altitudes where loss of cabin pressure would be fatal.

reported to be 75,000ft (22,860m), slightly below that of the earlier models.

The final version of the U-2 family is the TR-1. Changes from the U-2R standard are largely internal. The aircraft is heavier than the U-2R, and features an interchangeable nose plus a different pattern of dorsal UHF antenna. It carries an improved ECM system, also an advanced synthetic-aperture radar system (ASARS) based on the UPD-X sideways looking radar. Some aircraft were due to carry the Precision Emitter Location Strike System (PLSS), but plans to deploy this equipment have been cancelled.

The first example was a demilitarised airframe designated ER-2. First flown on 11 May 1982, it was delivered to NASA. It was followed by two two-seat TR-1Bs, then 25 single-seat TR-1As.

The TR-1 is now the only aircraft in the USAF inventory to use the 1950s-vintage J75 turbojet, and the resulting reliability and logistic-support problems have led the USAF to flight-test the aircraft with a General Electric F101-GE-F29 turbofan, a non-afterburning version of the engine used in the B-1B. Range, endurance and initial cruise altitude, would all be improved.

McDonnell Douglas RF-4C and -4E Phantom II

The first Phantom variant to sport a camera-packed nose was not the US Marine Corp's RF-4B but the USAF's RF-4C. The original YRF-4C prototypes were F-4Bs converted to the new role while still on the production line. A first flight on 8 August 1963 lead to the first of 503 production aircraft entering service in September 1964.

Two patterns of camera nose have been used on the RF-4C. The first was more angular, with a near flat underside to the camera fairing. The second had a rounded lower surface. Mounted under a small nose radome is the Goodyear APG-99 radar. Known to aircrew as the "forward looker", this allows the aircraft to fly in terrain-following mode. The lower part of the nose, including the chin fairing, housed optical cameras located on three stations. Film could be processed while the aircraft was in flight, and if necessary ejected in a cartridge which could be picked up by front-line personnel.

A Goodyear APQ-102A sideways looking radar recorded a broad strip of terrain on either side of the flight path on a film which could be processed after landing, and was backed up by an AAS-118 infra-red detecting set. The ALR-17 Countermeasures Receiving Set allows hostile radars to be identified and classified on the photo imagery, while the ALQ-161 normally carried on the centreline handles the elint task.

The USAF has spent more than $110 million in upgrading the APQ-99 radars of 312 RF-4s, and has installed the Litton Amecom ALQ-125 Tactical Electronic Reconnaissance (TEREC) and Ford Aerospace AVQ-26 Pave Tack laser designator/fire-control system aboard selected aircraft. A more drastic rework planned under the Advanced Tactical Air Reconnaissance System (ATARS) programme Tactical Air Command's "Tactical Reconnaissance Roadmap" would have replaced the aircraft's cameras with electro-optical sensors able to transmit real-time imagery via a digital data link.

Above: Without the protection offered by the white-painted external jamming pod, this large recce fighter would be vulnerable to modern SAM systems.

Above: The West German RF-4E fleet is currently being upgraded with an improved sensor suite, IR linescan, and a weapons-carrying capability.

The scheme was shelved in the spring of 1988. The long-term survivability of the aircraft was seen as too limited to warrant the modification.

The first of 46 RF-4Bs built for the USMC flew for the first time on 12 March 1965. These were generally similar to the RF-4C, combining the systems of the USAF aircraft with the airframe of the Navy's F-4B fighter. In an effort to extend RF-4B service life by a further eight years, a batch of 30 was reworked in 1978 under the Sensor Update and Refurbishment Effort (SURE). Equipment added included the APD-10 SLAR, AAD-5 infra-red reconnaissance set, and a data link.

The RF-4E is an export model operated by Germany, Greece, Iran, Israel, Japan and Turkey; approximately 150 were built. Spain is the sole export RF-4C operator. Many of the USAF sensors were highly classified, so could not be cleared for export. Customers ordering the RF-4E have in some cases had to accept an alternative equipment. Many operators are now updating their fleet. For example, Luftwaffe aircraft have been fitted with three Goodyear UPD-6 SLAR, which incorporate a data link able to transmit real-time radar data back to ground stations.

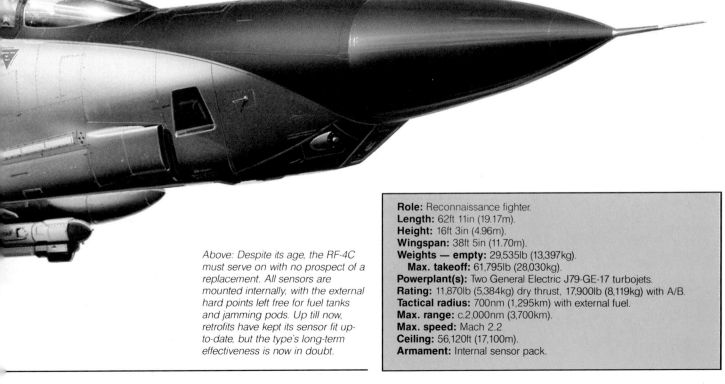

Above: Despite its age, the RF-4C must serve on with no prospect of a replacement. All sensors are mounted internally, with the external hard points left free for fuel tanks and jamming pods. Up till now, retrofits have kept its sensor fit up-to-date, but the type's long-term effectiveness is now in doubt.

Role: Reconnaissance fighter.
Length: 62ft 11in (19.17m).
Height: 16ft 3in (4.96m).
Wingspan: 38ft 5in (11.70m).
Weights — empty: 29,535lb (13,397kg).
　Max. takeoff: 61,795lb (28,030kg).
Powerplant(s): Two General Electric J79-GE-17 turbojets.
Rating: 11,870lb (5,384kg) dry thrust, 17,900lb (8,119kg) with A/B.
Tactical radius: 700nm (1,295km) with external fuel.
Max. range: c.2,000nm (3,700km).
Max. speed: Mach 2.2
Ceiling: 56,120ft (17,100m).
Armament: Internal sensor pack.

McDonnell Douglas RF-18D Hornet

By the late 1970s, the US Navy was faced with the growing obsolescence of its recon fleet. In October 1979, the service disbanded its last Rockwell RA-5C vigilante unit, leaving only the LTV RF-8G Crusader in service. Fighter versions of the F-8 had been retired from US service by 1975. The RF model was to serve on for another eight years, with the reserves retiring the type in 1987.

Although the Navy had its heart set on a new photo ship, this was not possible in the short term. The high cost of Tomcat rules out any dedicated ''RF-14'', while the basic F-18 would not enter service until the early 1980s, and would not be available for recce duties until the end of that decade.

As an interim measure, new sensors were packed into a pod.

Known as the Tactical Air Reconnaissance Pod System (TARPS), this could be carried under a standard F-14. Development started in 1976, leading to a first flight in 1977, and the authorisation of initial production examples in 1978. The system entered service in 1981, first with VF-84 ''Jolly Rogers'', with each Tomcat squadron receiving enough pods to allow several of its fighters to serve in the part-time recce role. During 1983, TARPS-equipped Tomcats flew missions over the Lebanon in support of the short-lived US military presence in that country.

One role performed by TARPS-equipped Tomcats deserves special mention in a book on spyplanes. Soon after the pod first entered service, it was used to photograph a highly-specialised intelligence target — Soviet intelligence-gathering aircraft found operating near US naval formations. Using the pod as an air-to-air camera, Tomcat crews took detailed photographs of these Soviet snoopers, helping US intelligence analysts catalogue and monitor the elint and camera gear fitted on these modified bombers. No doubt the

Role: Naval reconnaissance fighter.
Length: 56ft 0in (17.07m).
Height: 15ft 3.5in (4.66m).
Wingspan: 37ft 6in (11.43m).
Weights — empty: 23,050lb (10,455kg).
  Loaded: 36,710lb (16,650kg).
Powerplant(s): Two General Electric F404-GE-400 turbofans.
Rating: Approx. 16,000lb (7,260kg) in full afterburner.
Tactical radius: More than 400nm (740km).
Max. range: More than 2,000nm (3,700km).
Max. speed: More than Mach 1.8.
Ceiling: c.50,000ft (15,240m).
Armament: AIM-7 and AIM-9 missiles, one 20mm cannon and 17,000lb (7,700kg) ordnance.

Above: The Canadian markings on this RF-18 may raise a few eyebrows, but that nation is known to be considering a follow-on Hornet purchase. Could Canada become the first export customer for recce Hornets? At present, Canadian fighter squadrons have no dedicated recce aircraft.

Above: While the USAF ponders over possible replacements for the RF-4 Phantom, the US Navy has pressed ahead with the dedicated RF-18 recce version of Hornet.

Soviet crews were returning the favour, photographing the new pod and noting the tactics being developed for its use.

Sensors mounted in the TARPS pod include the KS-87B framing camera for forward or vertical coverage, the KA-99 low-altitude panoramic camera, and the Honeywell AAD-5A infra-red reconnaissance set. These sensors are controlled from the rear cockpit, while the data from the pod is projected into the aircraft HUD and cockpit CRT displays.

Detailed design and procurement of sensor payload of the RF-18 started in the early 1980s. Pod-mounted recce systems are inevitably a compromise, since the sensors are not firmly mounted to the aircraft structure. For the RF-18, the Navy planned to install a modified version of the TARPS system within the Hornet nose. Development of what became known as the Tactical Air Reconnaissance System (TARS) started in the early 1980s, the first RF-18 prototype flying in August 1984. The Navy originally hoped to buy 124 RF-18s, but this scheme was soon scaled back. Under current plans a total of 83 will be fielded with the first entering service in 1990.

Above: An RF-18D banks away from the camera to reveal the optical ports on its nose-mounted sensor bay. Until production airframes of this relatively new fighter could be spared for the recce role, the new sensors saw extensive service through the 1980s in pod-mounted form.

Mikoyan MiG-21 "Fishbed" H

Distinguishing between the various dedicated recce Fishbeds is difficult, and complicated by the fact that two variants (equipped with completely different equipment fits) both carry the Soviet designation MiG-21R. Faced with such problems it is little wonder that NATO has assigned all recce MiG-21s the common reporting name Fishbed H.

First recce Fishbed was probably a modified MiG-21F fitted in the early 1960s with a pallet-mounted camera installation beneath the cockpit floor in place of the normal cannon armament. Three cameras were carried — one forward oblique, one vertical and one panoramic. Despite the logic of this installation it was not adopted for Soviet or Warsaw Pact service.

Initial Warsaw Pact reconnaissance model was the MiG-21R. Based on the PFMA, this carries a centreline camera pod weighing about 1,100lb (500kg) on the centreline location reserved for the rarely carried GSh-23 gun pack. This contains several cameras (variously reported as "three" or even "five or six"), including forward oblique, vertical and panoramic types, all linked to the aircraft's navigation system and radar altimeter. There have been reports of a combined fuel/camera pod, but this seems unlikely. No armament is carried, but the aircraft apparently retains the R1L radar.

The same pod can also be used to carry elint sensors, a scheme first seen on some Polish AF aircraft. Glassfibre transparencies seen at the front and rear of both sides of the pod cover the antennas used for signal sampling. The pod probably contains recorders, since its links to the aircraft seem to be restricted to a connection which supplies electrical power. Wingspan is slightly increased due to the presence of wingtip ESM antennas. Some observers have suggested that the large antenna mounted within the dorsal spine is associated with a radio navaid, but in practice it probably serves to transmit reconnaissance data in near real time to ground stations or communications-relay aircraft.

The second version of the MiG-21R was exported to Egypt. Like its Warsaw Pact namesake, it is based on the -21PFMA fighter, but its sensor fit is internally mounted, and obviously based on that of the experimental MiG-21F installation. Like the 1960s design, this used three cameras mounted under the cockpit floor, but instead of mounting these sensors on a removable pallet, relies on a neat fixed installation. All three cameras are fixed to a large door located immediately aft of the nosewheel door. This hinges open along the starboard side for access to the sensors and film magazines. These Egyptian aircraft also carry wingtip pods fitted with forward and aft-facing helix antennas, but these may not be of Soviet origin.

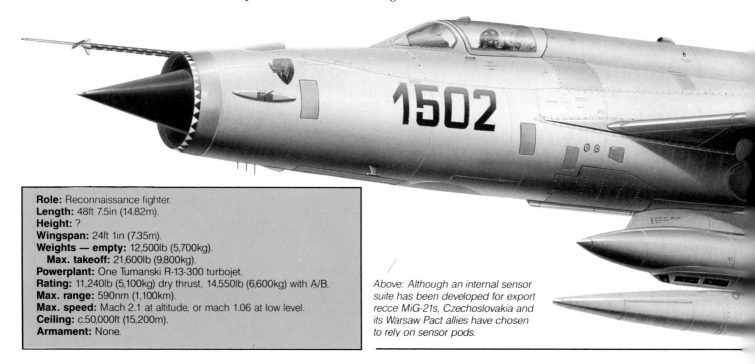

Above: Although an internal sensor suite has been developed for export recce MiG-21s, Czechoslovakia and its Warsaw Pact allies have chosen to rely on sensor pods.

Role: Reconnaissance fighter.
Length: 48ft 7.5in (14.82m).
Height: ?
Wingspan: 24ft 1in (7.35m).
Weights — empty: 12,500lb (5,700kg).
   Max. takeoff: 21,600lb (9,800kg).
Powerplant: One Tumanski R-13-300 turbojet.
Rating: 11,240lb (5,100kg) dry thrust, 14,550lb (6,600kg) with A/B.
Max. range: 590nm (1,100km).
Max. speed: Mach 2.1 at altitude, or mach 1.06 at low level.
Ceiling: c.50,000ft (15,200m).
Armament: None.

Above: This Polish Fishbed H (presumably photographed over the Baltic) carries an elint pod. The dark panels cover sampling antennas.

Mikoyan MiG-25R "Foxbat B, D and F"

The prototype Ye-26 flew for the first time in 1964, and examples made their public debut at the 1967 Domodedovo Air Show. The production Foxbat A interceptor had much larger vertical tail surfaces than the prototypes, and entered service in 1970. More than 300 were operational by the late 1970s, and exports were under way to selected customers. For armament, early production Foxbats may have carried the AA-5 Ash missile but the definitive weapon was the massive AA-6 Acrid.

From early in the programme, high priority was given to developing reconnaissance versions. First of these was the camera-equipped MiG-25R Foxbat B, which entered service in 1971. This had a low-drag conical nose, and a simpler wing of slightly reduced span and area. The leading edge of the fighter wing is less complex than that of the interceptor. The latter has compound sweep — 40° from the wing root to the outer pylon, then 38° to the wingtip. On the recce versions, a simple leading edge runs smoothly from root to tip, with a sweep angle of 42° throughout.

The redesigned nose contains five windows through which forward oblique, vertical and lateral cameras observe the ground. A small radome houses what is usually described as a Jay Bird radar. This J-band set is installed on late-model MiG-21s, but its usefulness in an unarmed reconnaissance aircraft seems doubtful. A small ventral fairing is almost certainly for a Doppler radar.

1975 saw the fielding of a second reconnaissance variant. Known to NATO as Foxbat D, this is an elint aircraft. The entire nose is devoted to elint systems (there are no cameras), and a large dielectric panel on the starboard side of the nose covers the antenna of an SLAR.

A later upgrade gave Foxbat B a degree of elint capability, adding a dielectric panel to the starboard side of the nose. Smaller than that on the D model, it too may house an SLAR antenna. Foxbat B and D aircraft are thought often to operate in pairs, with one providing optical coverage, and the other gathering elint information.

The little-known Foxbat F is based on the R31-engined Fox-

Left: For years, defence writers have speculated as to how NATO acquired this near-vertical photo of two recce Foxbats. An SR-71 or Israeli RF-4E mission to photograph aircraft on detachment to Egypt seems a likely explanation.

bat E interceptor. First seen in 1986, this is a defence-suppression aircraft armed with AS-11 Kegler anti-radiation missiles. This model also has a dielectric panel on the side of the nose, just aft of the radome.

Around 200 MiG-25Rs have been built, a mixture of B and D models. At least 33 have been exported to Algeria (6), India (6), Iraq (5), Libya (6) and Syria (10). Most are Foxbat B; the only known export operator of Foxbat D is thought to be Libya.

Role: Reconnaissance fighter.
Length: 78ft 1.75in (23.82m).
Height: 20ft 0.25in (6.10m).
Wingspan: 44ft (13.4m).
Weights — empty: 43,000lb (19,600kg).
  Max. takeoff: 73,650lb (33,400kg).
Powerplant(s): Two Tumanski R-31 turbojets.
Rating: 20,500lb (9,300kg) dry thrust, 27,011lb
  (12,250kg) with A/B.
Tactical radius: 610nm (1,130km).
Max. speed: Mach 2.83.
Ceiling: 80,000ft (24,400m).
Armament: None.

Below: The artist's drawing flatters the angular lines of a camera-equipped Foxbat B. The nose radome contains a small radar, perhaps intended as a navaid.

Above: A Foxbat B (foreground) and Foxbat D (rear) prepare for takeoff. Both are clean – external tanks would have to be jettisoned in a high-speed dash.

Below: This recce Foxbat is unusual in having the compound-sweep wing normally seen only on interceptor models. It was photographed around 1980.

Northrop RF-5A and RF-5E Tigereye

In October 1963, the USAF asked Northrop to develop a simple day-reconnaissance version of the F-5A, an aircraft whose capability would broadly match that of the RF-104G. On the resulting RF-5A, a modified nose section provided around three cubic feet of volume for the reconnaissance payload, which normally consisted of four KS-92 cameras.

First flight took place in May 1968, with deliveries to Norway, first customer for the type, starting a month later. The aircraft proved attractive to many F-5 users, and a total of 89 was built by the time production ended in June 1972.

Development of a reconnaissance version of the improved F-5E was long delayed. The RF-5E Tigereye project was not announced until early 1978. First aircraft fly was an aerodynamic prototype, which took to the air in January 1979. This flight tested the revised nose which had been devised to house a series of interchangeable sensors. Eight inches (20cm) longer than that of the basic fighter, it had a deeper profile, and incorporated optical windows, plus a large downward hinging door which gave access to the sensors.

Right: Malaysia was the first customer for the RF-5E Tigereye. but ordered only four examples. The windows in the sensor bay allow cameras and other sensors to scan from horizon to horizon.

Above: Although the RF-5E prototype was tested in USAF markings. it never saw US service. The sloped window in the extreme nose protects a single forward-facing camera.

A total of 26 cubic feet of space was available for sensors, almost nine times the volume available to the RF-5A.

In designing the new nose, Northrop eliminated one of the two 20mm cannon carried by the basic F-5E. The other was retained for self-defence, along with wingtip-mounted Sidewinder missiles.

The RF-5A had been a relatively simple aircraft, but for the -5E Northrop intended to create what amounted to a "mini-RF-4", an aircraft whose sensors were controlled by an integrated control system intended to minimise pilot workload, and whose configuration could be speedily modified for high-level, low-level or oblique-photography roles.

Mounted behind a sloped window in the extreme nose of the aircraft is a single KS-87D1 camera which can be fitted with a 6in (15cm) or 12in (30cm) lens. This was the only permanent part of the aircraft's sensor fit. A key element of the tactical flexibility offered by the RF-5E was the use of pallet-mounted sensors which could easily be changed as required by the individual mission.

Tigereye made its marketing debut at the 1979 Paris Air Show, by which time it had completed more than 60 flights and been test-flown by pilots from four nations. The RF-5E generated a lot of interest among F-5E users, with 31 nations evaluating the type over a three-year period. The first nation to order the new aircraft was Malaysia, which needed four.

This was followed by an order for 15 from Saudi Arabia.

The first Malaysian aircraft was rolled out at Palmdale in November 1982, and flew for the first time on 15 December. Deliveries started in the following summer. Despite a number of evaluations by other prospective users, no further orders were placed for the RF-5E.

Attrition is slowly reducing the numbers of RF-5s in service around the world. Current RF-5A users are Greece (8), Morocco (1), South Korea (6), Thailand (4), and Turkey (20). Norway has phased out its fleet of around a dozen. Malaysia now has only two RF-5Es, while Saudi Arabia has 12.

Role: Reconnaissance fighter.
Length: 48ft 1in (14.65m).
Height: 13ft 4in (4.07m).
Wingspan: 26ft 8in (8.13m).
Weights — empty: c.9,800lb (4,445kg).
Max. takeoff: ?
Powerplant(s): Two General Electric J58-GE-21B turbojets.
Rating: 5,000lb (2,268kg) with A/B.
Tactical radius: 350nm (648km) at low altitude; 595nm (1,102km) at high alt.
Max. range: 1,545nm (2,8630km) with external tanks.
Max. speed: Mach 1.64 at altitude.
Ceiling: 51,800ft (15,790m).
Armament: Sensor pallet plus two AIM-9 Sidewinders.

Below: In the mid-1970s, Northrop developed this interchangeable four-camera nose for use on Saudi Arabian F-5E fighters. The dedicated RF-5E was purchased in the 1980s.

Panavia Tornado GR.1 and ECR

At first there were no plans for dedicated reconnaissance versions of Tornado. The existing IDS version was expected to handle the role. For the German Navy and Italian Air Force, MBB developed a suitable reconnaissance pod. Carried on the aircraft centreline, this 840lb (380kg) unit contains a Texas Instruments infra-red line scanner, and two wide-angle Zeiss cameras. The LHOV camera may be focused to any distance from 300 yards (300m) to infinity during the mission, or may be left at a fixed setting. The LLDC camera provides horizon-to-horizon coverage. Mounted at the rear of the pod is the reconnaissance interface system. This controls the overall system, co-ordinating aircraft and sensor data.

Britain's RAF decided not to rely on "home-grown" IR technology, opting to rely on an internally mounted equipment pack which fits into the aircraft's gun bays. This contains three IR line scanners — a single wide-angle unit plus two sideways looking high-definition thermal scanners. Working together, the three provide horizon-to-horizon coverage. Data from these instruments can be recorded on video tape, and monitored by the aircraft navigator. Development of a real-time datalink seems to have followed on a later timescale, so this equipment is not yet in service. The first unit to deploy the new variant was 2 Squadron in West Germany, which formed in the winter of 1988-9, with the aircraft replacing Sepecat Jaguars fitted with centreline recce pods.

Development of the Electronic Combat and Reconnaissance (ECR) version for the West German Luftwaffe started in 1986. Flight trials started in August 1988 using a converted Tornado IDS prototype, and the test fleet eventually numbered four.

The production aircraft were ordered as part of the seventh production batch, and deliveries are now under way. The 35 ECR aircraft currently on order will serve with 4/JaboG 32 at Lechfeld and 2/JaboG 38 at Jever. Tornado ECR carries an

Left: During anti-radar attacks using HARM missiles, the ECR would rely on the underwing jamming pod (stbd) and chaff dispenser (port) for self-protection.

Role: Multirole combat aircraft.
Length: 54ft 10.25in (16.72m).
Height: 19ft 6.25in (5.95m).
Wingspan: 28ft 2.5in-45ft 7.5in (8.60-13.91m).
Weights — empty: 31,065lb (14,091kg).
  Loaded: 45,000lb (20,410kg).
  Max. takeoff: c.60,000lb (27,200kg).
Powerplant(s): Two Turbo-Union RB.199 Mk.103 turbofans.
Rating: 9,656lb (4,380kg) dry thrust, 16,920lb (7,675kg) in A/B.
Tactical radius: 750nm (1,390km) hi-lo-hi with heavy weapons load.
Max. range: c.2,100nm (3,890km).
Max. speed: Mach 2.2 clean, Mach 0.92 with external stores.
Ceiling: ?
Armament: 18,000lb (8,165kg) of ordnance plus two 27mm Mauser cannon.

Right: Flight trials of Tornado ECR prototypes started in August 1988. Several years of testing will be needed to clear the aircraft for operational use.

emitter-location system, a low/medium-altitude reconnaissance system consisting of an FLIR and IR linescanner, and an Odin digital datalink. External payload would normally be jamming pods, AGM-88 HARM anti-radiation missiles, and external fuel tanks. To make room for the new avionics, the aircraft's twin 27mm Mauser cannon have been deleted. Self-protection is limited to two AIM-9L Sidewinders plus ECM/flare dispensers.

The combat role of the ECR would be reconnaissance, air-defence suppression, and strikes against command and control facilities. It could be used to reconnoitre suitable routes for follow-on strike formations, and to locate radar, SAM or communications targets for them.

The UK has no plans to procure the ECR. Italy has announced plans to buy up to 16, and should have signed a contract by the end of 1989. Instead, the Italian Air Force decided to await the results of flight trials by the Luftwaffe. The type could prove attractive to export customers, however, and is being offered to the USAF as a basis for a possible replacement for the F-4G Wild Weasel.

Saab-Scania SF37 and SH37 Viggen

Development of specialised reconnaissance versions of the Viggen was ordered in 1972. Most air forces would have been content to order a single recce variant, but the Flyvapnet ordered two — the SF37 for general reconnaissance duties, and the SH37 for maritime surveillance. Both are powered by the same Volvo Flygmotor RM8A turbofan as used in the AJ.37 strike and SK.37 trainer aircraft.

The first version to fly was the SF37. This may be easily recognised by a redesigned nose section with no nose radome, but a chin fairing for cameras and other sensors. The first example flew in May 1973, and the type entered service to replace the S35E Draken. The first SH37 flew in June 1975. This variant retains a nose-mounted surveillance radar, supplementing this with underwing pods.

A total of 28 SF37s and 26 SH37s were built by the time that production ended in February 1981. When the final aircraft — an SK37 – left the Linkoping production line, this concluded the assembly of RM8A-powered Viggens. The airframes which followed were RM8B-powered JA37 interceptors.

The chin fairing of the SF37 is used to carry low and high-level optical cameras, plus IR sensors. These are supplemented by external pods carrying cameras, night-illumination systems, or an infra-red line scanner. The pod for the latter is made by FFV, and is known as Red Baron.

The radar within the nose of the SH37 is a modified version of the Ericsson PS-37/A fitted to the AJ37 strike aircraft. This is used as a long-range surveillance sensor, so its display is fitted with a camera. Optical target surveillance is handled by an underwing pod containing a long-distance camera.

A fuel tank is often carried on the centreline of reconnaissance Viggens, leaving the inboard wing pylons free for sensor pods, and the outboard for ECM pods or Sidewinder missiles for self-defence. Sidewinder, known as Rb.24 in Swedish service, is available in several versions including the AIM-9L, and L.M. Ericsson has developed an optical proximity fuze for use on earlier models.

Most of the SF37 and SH37 fleet is still operational, serving with three wings of the RSwAF.AF — F13 at Norrkoping, F17 at Ronneby and F21 at Lulea. All three units fly the SF and SH models. F13 includes a dedicated SH squadron, but F17 and F21 have squadrons operating a mix of the two models. Although primarily tasked with maritime surveillance, the SH37 has a secondary attack role. This has been reported as ground attack, but is more likely to be maritime strike.

Role: Reconnaissance aircraft.
Length: 53ft 5.7in (16.3m).
Height: 19ft 0.25in (5.8m).
Wingspan: 34ft 9.25in (10.60m).
Weights — empty: ?
   Loaded: c.33,070lb (15,000kg).
   Max. takeoff: c.44,090lb (20,000kg).
Powerplant(s): One Volvo Flygmotor RM8A turbofan.
Rating: 14,750lb (6,690kg) dry thrust, 25,990lb (11,790kg) with A/B.
Max. speed: Mach 2+ at altitude, Mach 1.2 at 330ft (100m).
Armament: Internal pod-mounted sensors plus AIM-9 or other ordnance.

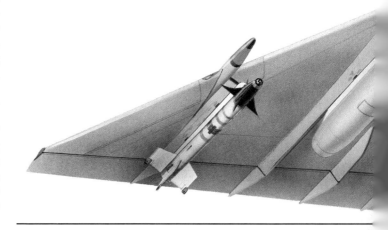

Left: While the SF-37 can be easily recognised thanks to its distinctive chisel nose, the SH-37 retains the original radome. In addition to its surveillance radar housed in the nose, various recce pods can be carried on external hardpoints.

Left: On the SF37, a camera or FLIR pod can supplement the sensors packed into the nose bay. On the maritime-recce SH37 model, the nose carries a radar, so the pod is needed if EO coverage is required. The aircraft shown here carries underwing pods for jamming (starboard) and chaff (port).

Boeing RC-135

Ten TF33-P-9-powered KC-135 aircraft delivered to the USAF in 1964-5 were fitted out by Martin Aircraft of Baltimore to act as RC-135B reconnaissance platforms. A 1967 rework added SLAR cheeks to the sides of the forward fuselage and deleted the boom operator's compartment to make way for a camera bay. All have since been converted to the RC-135U or -135V standard.

Four KC-135A tankers were rebuilt in 1962-3 as RC-135Ds, receiving a thimble-shaped nose radome (which was to become a standard fitting on all later models unless otherwise noted), and narrow fairings for SLAR on the forward fuselage. The three survivors were restored to tanker configuration between 1975 and 1979.

A 1967-8 rebuilt converted six C-135Bs into RC-135Ms. Externally, this looked similar to the D, but with teardrop fairings mounted on the aft fuselage rather than a SLAR. Some have been rebuilt as RC-135Ws.

Two C-135Bs were modified to create the RC-135S. In addition to the large teardrop fairings first seen on the -135M, these have smaller teardrop fairings at the base of the vertical fin, and dipole antennas arranged around the front fuselage. A 1972 rebuild introduced three large round windows on the right side of the fuselage, and a black anti-reflective finish on the upper surface of the right wing and on the wing pods and pylons. These features are probably associated with an electro-optical sensor used to observe Soviet re-entry vehicles during ballistic missile tests.

The KC-135R variant is unusual in that it has the designation ''KC'' rather than ''RC'', and that the four KC-135s known to have been rebuilt to this standard were not done as a batch, but individually in 1963, 1970, then two in 1971. Features in-

Above: Despite the poor lighting conditions, the thimble nose radome, large cheek fairing, and the probe at the right wingtip identify this as an RC-135V.

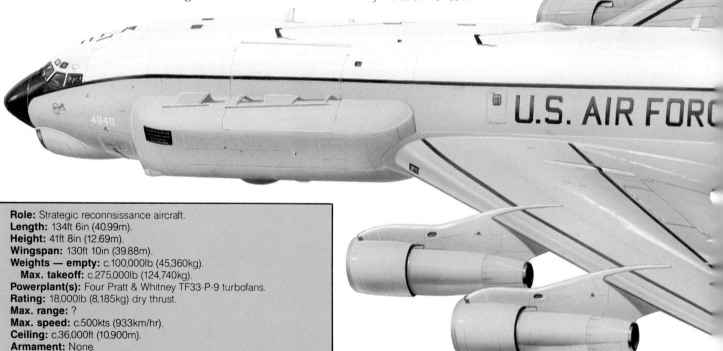

Role: Strategic reconnsissance aircraft.
Length: 134ft 6in (40.99m).
Height: 41ft 8in (12.69m).
Wingspan: 130ft 10in (39.88m).
Weights — empty: c.100,000lb (45,360kg).
   Max. takeoff: c.275,000lb (124,740kg).
Powerplant(s): Four Pratt & Whitney TF33-P-9 turbofans.
Rating: 18,000lb (8,185kg) dry thrust.
Max. range: ?
Max. speed: c.500kts (933km/hr).
Ceiling: c.36,000ft (10,900m).
Armament: None.

clude the thimble nose radome, a "towel-rail" dorsal antenna on the forward fuselage, and -135M-style "teardrop" fairings.

A 1971 rebuild of three RC-135Cs created today's RC-135U fleet. The original pattern of nose clearly indicates the aircraft's ancestry, but in other respects these are highly modified, having gained a chin-mounted radome, dipole antennas on the forward fuselage, large SLAR "cheeks", a small ventral radome, reworked wingtips housing antennas, two -135T-style wire antennas, an ovoid fairing at the top of the rudder, and an extended tailcone.

Seven RC-135Cs were given similar rebuilds between 1973 and 1977 to create the -135V, while another was made by modifying a single -135U. Broadly similar to the -135V, this lacks the earlier aircraft's chin and ventral radomes, dipole antennas, wingtip and rudder fairings and extended tailcone. New features are the standard "thimble" nose, and large ventrally mounted blade antennas.

Below: The RC-123U was developed under the Combat Scent programme as a means of locating and monitoring Soviet-type SAM sites. It first saw service during the Vietnam War.

Right: One of the 55th Strategic Reconnaissance Wing's eight RC-135Vs. The new -135W model is similar in appearance, and a single -135X has recently been reported.

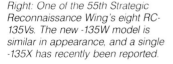

General Dynamics/ Grumman EF-111A Raven

Developed to replace the Douglas EB-66 electronic-warfare aircraft, the EF-111A combines the airframe and engines of the General Dynamics F-111A with the Eaton AIL ALQ-99 EW suite of the US Navy's Grumman EA-6B Prowler. Work on converting two F-111As as prototypes for the EF-111A Tactical Jamming System (TJS) aircraft started in January 1975, leading to a first flight on 10 March 1977. The task was given not to GD but to Grumman. The Long Island company was familiar with the F-111, having developed the unsuccessful FB-111B fighter variant in the 1960s.

Being the earliest version of the aircraft to enter service, the F-111A was coming to the end of its life as a combat aircraft, but enough airframes were available to make a rebuild for the new role feasible. The EW suite needed drastic modification, however.

The EA-6B carries a crew of four — a pilot plus three system operators — but the GD warplane had only a two-place cockpit. Automation would have to take the place of two of the three system operators. Flight testing on the revised

ALQ-99E system uncovered some problems, but tests went smoothly enough to allow the USAF to agree in November 1979 to a programme which would rebuild a total of 42 ex-USAF F-111A aircraft as EW platforms.

Between 1980 and 1985, Grumman stripped these aircraft down, rebuilding them to a build standard with an estimated fatigue life of around 8,000 hours. This added a new avionics bay in the lower fuselage, a large ventral "canoe" fairing, plus

Role: Electronic warfare aircraft.
Length: 76ft 0in (23.16m).
Height: 20ft 0in (6.10m).
Wingspan: 31ft 11in (9.74m) swept, 63ft 0in (19.2m) unswept.
Weights — empty: 55,275lb (25,072kg).
   Loaded: 70,000lb (31,700kg).
   Max. takeoff: 88,948lb (40,356kg).
Powerplant(s): Two Pratt & Whitney TF30-P-3 turbofans.
Rating: 18,500lb (8,390kg) with A/B.
Tactical radius: 807nm (1,495km) in the escort role.
Max. speed: 1,227kts (2,272km/hr).
Ceiling: 45,000ft (13,700m).
Armament: None.

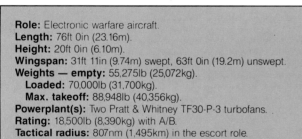

Above: The fairing at the top of the fin houses EW receivers and antennas. The round dome-shaped window covers a sensor for the ALR-23 infra-red warning receiver.

Below: Apart from the fin-top fairing, this general view of an EF-111A gives little clue as to the magnitude of the rebuild from the earlier F-111A standard.

a Prowler-style fintop fairing. These changes created the internal volume needed to house the electronics and antennas of the ALQ-99E and a Sanders ALQ-137 CW deception jammer for self-protection.

The USAF took delivery of its first EF-111A in 1981, and deployment to Western Europe came in 1984. More than a year before the final example was handed over in December 1985, Eaton AIL and General Dynamics were given a $61

Above: The canoe-shaped fairing below the forward fuselage was part of the rebuild which converted the original weapons bay into housing for ALQ-99E EW electronics.

million contract to upgrade the ALQ-99E. In its basic form this system covers frequencies from VHF to J-band, pumping out enough jamming power to be effective at ranges of up to 124nm (230km). The proposed upgrade was intended to deal with what was described as ''fast-moving technology and the rapid upgrading of many foreign air defences''.

Cost overruns and a badly slipping schedule doomed this programme, which was cancelled in June 1988. The only upgrading currently being applied to the aircraft is the Avionics Modernisation Programme. This will improve the cockpit, upgrade the radar (the rebuilt aircraft had retained the originally fitted APQ-110 terrain following radar and APQ-160 navigation radar), and fit a laser-gyro inertial navigation system and a GPS satnav receiver.

Given that the aircraft could remain in service until around the year 2010 some further modernisation is needed. Possible upgrades include the installation of the new receiver/processor developed for the USN's EA-6B, a new low-band radar and communications jammer, or AGM-88 HARM anti-radiation missiles. The ALQ-137 deception jammer could be upgraded to the improved -189 form or replaced by a unit from another manufacturer.

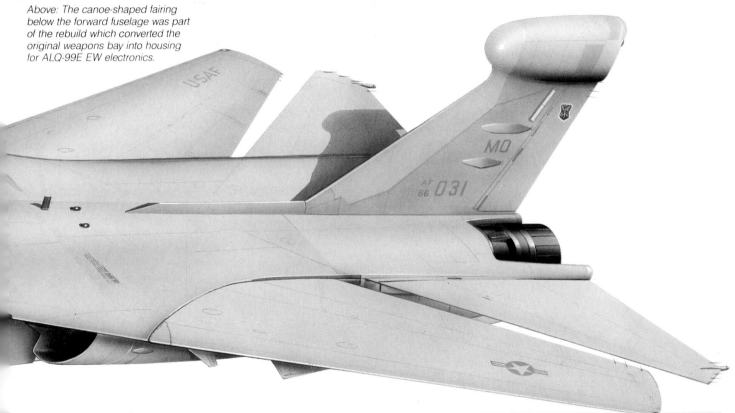

Ilyushin Il-20 "Coot-A"

Production of the Il-18 airliner ended around 1970, but a new military version designated "Coot-A" by NATO was first sighted in 1978. This seems to be a Soviet equivalent of the RC-135 — a proven transport adapted to carry a wide range of reconnaissance and elint sensors.

The location and number of fuselage windows make it clear that the aircraft is essentially a military adaption of the airliner, and almost certainly the result of rebuilding obsolescent low-hour ex-airline or ex-military airframes. This probably involved a major rebuild of the forward fuselage to add the large equipment housings which are the most obvious external features of the modified aircraft. These include a large cylindrical container carried beneath the forward fuselage. Approximately 34ft 6in (10.5m) long and 3ft 9in (1.15m) in diameter, it houses a large SLAR antenna. Published reports suggest that this equipment operates in J-band.

Smaller canoe-shaped fairings on either side of the forward fuselage just aft of the flight deck pose a minor mystery. These

Above: The Il-20 may not look as attractive as the USAF's RC-135, but despite the noise and vibration from the turboprops, it's a practical platform for recce and elint duties.

Right: The radomes, antennas and fairings on the fuselage of the Il-20 led the UK magazine Flight International *to nickname the aircraft "the snoop Coot".*

are about 14ft (4.25m) long and 3ft (0.9m) deep, and would at first sight be suitable for SLAR antennas, but it seems unlikely that the aircraft would need two radars of this type. A dielectric fairing occupies the aft two-thirds of their length, confirming that these fairings do house elint electronics, but the existence of a small door about a third of the way from the forward end betrays the presence of sideways-looking cameras or electro-optical sensors.

Many antennas have been added, including two prominent antennas on the roof of the forward fuselage. These fittings are about 1ft 6in (0.5m) high, and tapering from 4ft 6in (1.4m) down to 2ft 3in (0.7m). A circular dielectric blister is mounted directly under the rear of the wing roots, while aft of the blister are two cylindrical housings, then an array of five stub antennas.

Examination of the fuselage shows the presence of several light-coloured rectangular panels, three on either side of the aft fuselage and one mounted in the starboard rear door of the cargo hold. These are probably made from glassfibre, and act as radio transparencies for wide-angle microwave antennas used to sample any radar and radio radar transmissions in the area through which the Coot-A is patrolling.

Fittings under the rear fuselage just ahead of the tailplane have been interpreted as chutes (presumably for chaff or flares). It is also possible that they are outlets for air used to cool the avionics.

Around 20 aircraft have been converted to the Coot-A configuration. These operate over the Baltic and Norwegian Sea. Most surprising feature of the programme is the absence of variants. The USAF seems to have an almost uncontrollable urge to modify its RC-135 fleet, yet Coot is virtually unchanged after ten years of service.

Above: A Western interceptor must have crept uncomfortably close to this Il-20 in order to photograph the cluster of three radomes which forms part of its EW installation. They may contain steerable antennas for communicating with warships.

Role: Maritime reconnaissance aircraft.
Length: 117ft 9in (35.9m).
Height: 33ft 4in (10.17m).
Wingspan: 122ft 9.25in (37.42m).
Weights — empty: ?.
   Max. takeoff: c.140,000lb (64,000kg).
Powerplant(s): Four Ivchenko AI-24M turboprops.
Rating: 4,250shp (3,169kW).
Max. speed: 364kts (675km/hr).
Ceiling: c.33,000ft (10,000m).
Armament: None.

Lockheed EC-130E, G, H, and Q Hercules

The huge cargo cabin of the C-130 makes it an obvious basis for specialised electronics roles, and the type has been used to create aircraft for elint, jamming, and command/control. The first to be fielded were the C-130A-II and -130B-II, both thought to have been elint aircraft. About a dozen of each were created by converting transports, and were restored to the cargo role in the early 1970s.

Several different aircraft seem to have shared the EC-130E designation. Originally known as the C-130E-II, the first was an airborne fighter control centre developed for use during the Vietnam War. It can be recognised by the presence of large air scoops on either side of the forward fuselage.

The second type of EC-130E was built in 1979, and carries a USC-15 Airborne Battlefield Command and Control Centre (ABCCC) capsule in its hold — a 40ft (12m) long shelter housing communications equipment and a staff of between 12 and 16. This pattern of EC-130E currently serves with the 7th Airborne Command and Control Squadron at Keesler AFB, Mississippi.

A second version of the EC-130 codenamed "Coronet Solo II" is operated from Middletown, Pennsylvania, by the 193rd Special Operations Group of the Air National Guard. This version is instantly recognisable by the presence of huge blade antennas beneath the other panels of both wings, plus another mounted at the junction of the leading edge of the vertical fin. Two underwing pods located close to the each wingtip, and a system under the rear fuselage can each deploy long trailing-wire HF antennas. Two large underwing pods — one between each pair of engines — house the heat exchangers which are needed to cool the electronics equipment. Some

Right: Probably the most grotesque Hercules variant ever fielded, the EC-130 Coronet Solo II is a command and control aircraft for use during special operations. The huge panels hanging downwards under each wing, and forward of the fin, house antennas.

Below: In flight, this US Navy EC-130Q TACAMO aircraft of VQ-4 trails a 6 miles (10km) wire antenna used for communication with ballistic missile submarines. It will be replaced by the new Boeing E-6A, the final model of the long-estabished 707 series.

sources suggest that these aircraft are used for electronic surveillance, others suggest a command and control function is more likely.

The EC-130G was the US Navy's original TACAMO (TAke Charge And Move Out) communications aircraft used for survivable communications with the ballistic missile submarines (SSBNs) of the US Navy. Four were built, and were followed by 16 EC-130Q follow-on TACAMO aircraft with better equipment and improved crew accommodation. They are now being replaced by the E-6A derivative of the Boeing 707 airliner.

One TACAMO aircraft orbits over the Atlantic at all times, another over the Pacific. The aircraft is fitted with a 6.2 mile (10km) long trailing-wire antenna for VLF radio communications. When transmitting, the aircraft banks in a continuous circle, so that the wire hangs near-vertically for most of its length.

The EC-130H entered service in 1982 and serves with the 41st Electronic Combat Squadron at Davis-Monthan AFB, Arizona, and the 66th Electronic Combat Wing at Sembach AB, West Germany. A total of 16 were built to carry the classified Compass Call, an EW system designed to jam communications links.

Some deficiencies were noted in the system as originally fielded, but Project 2462 (Compass Call Development) was initiated to make the EW suite more powerful, fast-reacting, and able to handle multiple threats simultaneously. These improvements were added to the aircraft in the late 1980s, and are expected to maintain the aircraft's effectiveness well into the 1990s.

For a quarter of a century, the US Navy used the specialised WC-130 for weather reconnaissance duties such as the tracking of typhoons. By the early 1980s, satellites had taken over most of this work, and the WC-130 fleet was responsible for only some 15 per cent of typhoon warnings. The last WC-130 unit was disbanded in September 1987.

Role: EW aircraft.
Length: 97ft 9in (29.79m).
Height: 38ft 3in (11.66m).
Wingspan: 132ft 7in (40.41m).
Weights — empty: 76,469lb (34,686kg).
   Loaded: 155,000lb (70,310kg).
   Max. takeoff: 175,000lb (79,380kg).
Powerplant(s): Four Allison T56-A-15 turboprops.
Rating: 4,508shp (3,363kW).
Max. speed: 325kts (602km/hr).
Ceiling: 33,000ft (10,060m).
Armament: None.

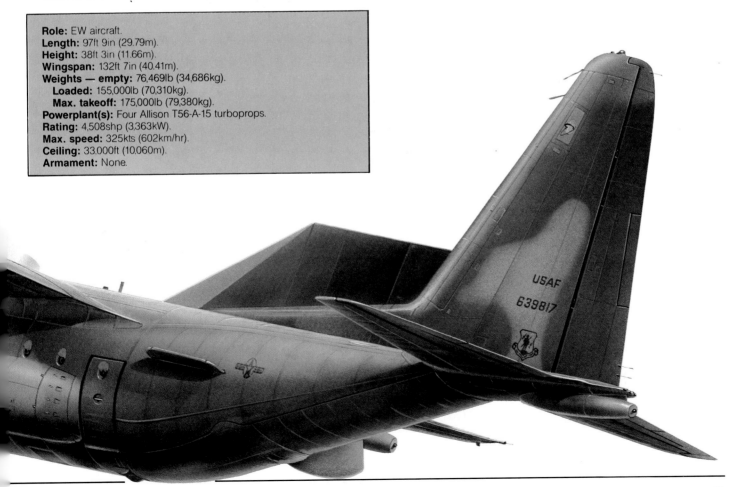

Lockheed EP-3E Orion

In the 1950s and 1960s the US Navy relied on the piston-engined EC-121M (formerly designated WV-2Q) for the elint mission, but by the 1960s a replacement was needed for these modified Lockheed Constellations. Two P-3B were converted into EP-3B elint aircraft and delivered to Fleet Air Reconnaissance Squadron VQ-1 in 1969. Along with ten P-3A, they were rebuilt to the definitive EP-3E standard in the early 1970s.

Obvious external changes are the deletion of the MAD ''sting'' and the installation of dielectric equipment fairings above and below the rear fuselage, a dorsal radome mounted just ahead of the wing leading edge, plus an array of wire and blade antennas.

Above: Festooned in elint radomes and with only simple national markings, a US Navy EP-3E patrols above the clouds, sampling radar signals from Soviet warships.

Role: Elint aircraft.
Length: 116ft 10in (35.61m).
Height: 33ft 8.5in (10.27m).
Wingspan: 99ft 8in (30.37m).
Weights — empty: ?
   Max. takeoff: 142.000lb (64,400kg).
Powerplant(s): Four Allison T56-A-14 turboprops.
Rating: 4,910shp (3,661kW).
Tactical radius: 1,346nm (2,494km) with 3hr on station.
Max. speed: 411kts (761km/hr).
Ceiling: 28,300ft (8,625m).
Armament: None.

The aircraft carries a crew of 15 — a flight crew, relief flight crew, and system operators. The latter operates an extensive suite of elint sensors.

The exact nature of this suite may well vary from aircraft to aircraft. Main systems identified as being carried by the EP-3E are the United Technologies ALQ-110 Aries/Big Look sigint system, the GTE ALR-60 Deep Well communications intercept system, an E-Systems ALD-8 DF system, the Loral ALQ-78 ESM receiver (now being replaced by the newer ALR-77), an Argo Systems ALR-52 broadband frequency-measuring receiver, thought to cover from 0.5 to 18GHz, and the Hughes AAR-37 IR receiver.

Some sources claim that the Magnavox ARR-81 airborne sigint system has also been carried by the EP-3. This equipment can be fitted with any two of three receivers designed to cover 1KHz-32MHz, 20-500MHz, and 500MHz-2GHz respectively. Another system thought to have served on some EP-3 aircraft is IBM's ASQ-171 automatic elint collection system. This covers the spectrum from A-band to J-band, but has the capability of being extended to cover K-band.

Such is the small size of the USN's elint fleet that some of these systems were built in only small quantities. Production run of the ALR-60 Deep Well is reported to have been only seven systems.

Two other Orion variants have been built for surveillance and survey duties. Under the US Naval Oceanographic Office's Project Magnet, a single RP-3D in service with VXN-8 was used in the 1970s to map the earth's magnetic field. Four specialised WP-3As were built in 1975-6 for weather reconnaissance. These replaced the earlier WC-121N version of the Constellation, and carry a dorsal radome similar to that sported by the EP-3E. Two civil-registered WP-3Bs were used by the National Oceanic and Atmospheric Administration for environmental research.

Above: The "Roadrunner" nose insignia and "Project Magnet" inscription on the tail fin of this Orion identify it as the RP-3D magnetic-survey aircraft.

Below: US Navy equivalent of the USAF's RC-135 is the little-known EP-3E Orion. Only 12 were built, and their role is thought to be the tracking of Soviet naval formations.

McDonnell Douglas F-4G Phantom II

The first anti-radar version of the Phantom was created in the late 1960s by the Wild Weasel 4 programme. A total of 36 F-4Cs were rebuilt to a standard unofficially known as the EF-4C. Delivered from 1969 onwards, serving with the 81st TFW at Spangdahlem AB in West Germany, and the 67th TFS at Kadena AB in Okinawa.

An attempt was made in the 1970s to develop a Weasel based on the F-4D, but details of the EF-4D Weasel programme are vague. Various accounts of the programme give conflicting timescales, equipment fits, and aircraft serial numbers.

From 1978 onwards, the EF-4C was replaced in front-line service by the newer F-4G, so was relegated to service with training units. The survivors were eventually issued to the ANG as F-4Cs.

To create the definitive F-4G, the USAF decided to rebuild existing fighters. The model chosen was the F-4E. A batch of 116 selected aircraft with long fatigue lives was earmarked for conversion. A rebuild process carried out at the USAF's Air Logistic Centre at Ogden AFB, Utah, saw these aircraft stripped of their 20mm cannon and fighter avionics, then fitted out with the new mission systems based around the APR-38. A revised chin fairing houses many of the system's antennas, while others are located in a new fairing at the top of the vertical fin.

Radar signals from enemy emitters are detected, analysed and compared with the extensive on-board library of threat signatures contained in the aircraft's central computer. The computer can be reprogrammed at squadron level, being given updated software which reflects the latest threat information and tactics. Frequency coverage of the APR-38 is classified. One Western estimate suggests that the system covers from A band to J (0.1-18GHz), while a Soviet source claims a more realistic minimum frequency of 0.6GHz (low to mid C band).

The first converted aircraft was rolled out on 28 April 1978, and production continued at a rate of three per month until all 116 had been delivered. A total of 96 were delivered to operational users, with 20 being kept for training or as attrition replacements. A small follow-on order was placed in the mid-1980s to replace some of the ten or so aircraft lost by then.

Like the earlier F-100 and F-105 based Weasels, the F-4G is being upgraded to keep abreast of new threats. Initially, these updates were relatively modest, for example, better navaids. The Wild Weasel 7 scheme started in the early 1980s was a more ambitious effort. Phase I expanded the on-board

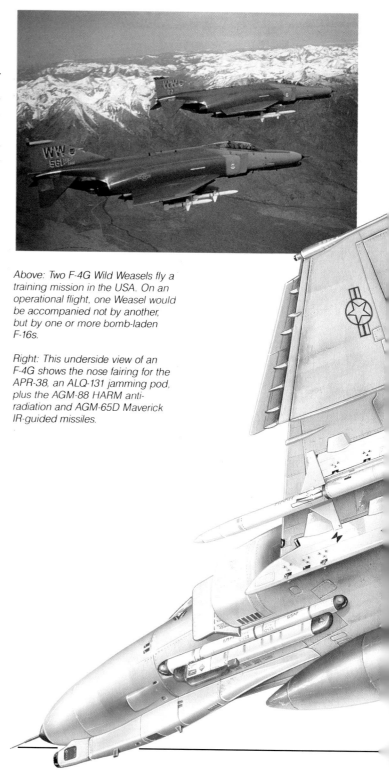

Above: Two F-4G Wild Weasels fly a training mission in the USA. On an operational flight, one Weasel would be accompanied not by another, but by one or more bomb-laden F-16s.

Right: This underside view of an F-4G shows the nose fairing for the APR-38, an ALQ-131 jamming pod, plus the AGM-88 HARM anti-radiation and AGM-65D Maverick IR-guided missiles.

computer capability, and systems fitted with new processor are designated APR-47. Phase II would have improved the frequency coverage to match developments in Soviet-bloc equipment. New receivers were test-flown in the mid-1980s, but technical problems led to cancellation of this programme.

The Wild Weasel 6 programme has looked at creating a new anti-radar aircraft, probably based on the F-15 or F-16, but the ability to mount AGM-88 Harm anti-radiation missiles on modern fighters such as the latest models of the F-16 will probably spell the end of the Wild Weasel concept.

Role: Anti-radar aircraft.
Length: 63ft 0in (19.2m).
Height: 16ft 6in (5.03m).
Wingspan: 38ft 5in (11.70m).
Weights — empty: ?
  Max. takeoff: 61,795lb (28,030kg).
Powerplant(s): Two General Electric J79-GE-17 turbojets.
Rating: 11,870lb (5,384kg) dry thrust, 17,900lb (8,119kg) with A/B
Max range: c.2,000nm (3,700km).
Max. speed: Mach 2.2
Ceiling: 56,120ft (17,100m).
Armament: 16,000lb (7,250kg) of ordnance.

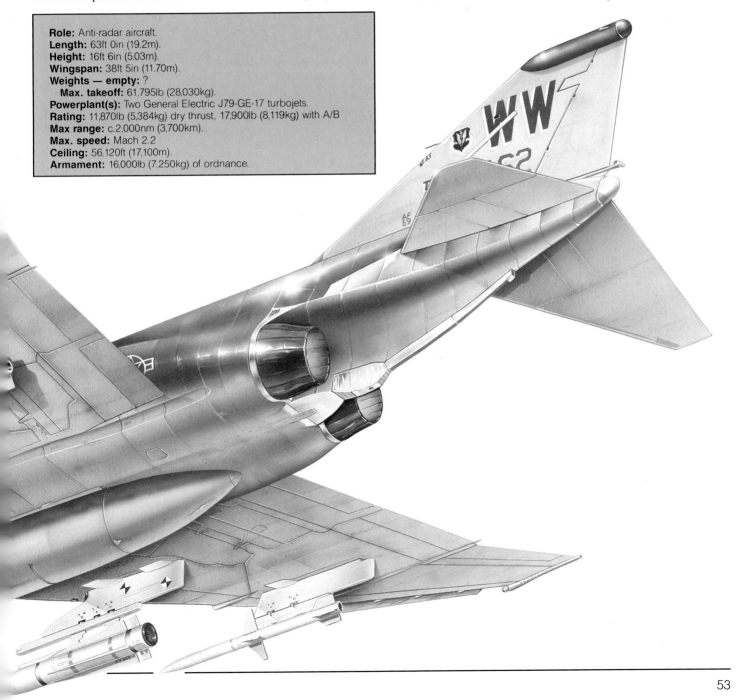

Sikorsky EH-60C Quickfix IIB Blackhawk

This EW version of Blackhawk is the US Army's latest solution to the problem of locating and jamming enemy communications systems. The Quickfix programme started in the mid-1970s, and originally used Bell UH-1 helicopters fitted with the GR-9 intercept receiver and a TLQ-27A jammer.

By the early 1980s, these Quickfix 1A aircraft had been replaced by the EH-1H Quickfix IB, which carried the more effective TLQ-17A jammer. These were followed by the EH-1X Quickfix IIA, equipped with an ALQ-151 intercept/jamming suite able to cover frequencies between 2 and 76MHz, and emitting between 40 and 150W of jamming power probably modulated with noise.

Quickfix IIB is based on the EH-60 version of the Blackhawk. The YEH-60A prototype first flew on 24 September 1981, and the production EH-60C version entered service in the late 1980s. Details of the avionics are classified (note that our specifications are for the EH-60A) but the aircraft is probably fitted with an improved version of the ALQ-151. A large antenna is fitted beneath the rear fuselage on a swing-down mounting, while four small dipoles on the tail boom are probably used for direction-finding intercepted signals.

The EH-60C has a crew of five — pilot, co-pilot, crew chief, and two EW operators. The operators are seated at consoles in the front part of the cabin, while the crew chief sits behind them in order to oversee and co-ordinate their individual activities.

Any EW aircraft would be a high-priority target in wartime, so the EH-60C carries a self-protection system known as the Aircraft Survivability Equipment (ASE). This probably consists of an APR-39(V)2 radar-warning receiver and several M-130 chaff/flare dispensers mounted on the tailboom. The engines are fitted with IR suppressors.

Although the Army wanted to deploy 77 aircraft, the programme seems to have ended in 1988 with delivery of the sixty-sixth example. These aircraft are likely to remain in service until the late 1990s, when they are due to be replaced by the Common Heliborne Jammer, a system due to enter development in 1992.

The planned EH-60B was test-flown as a radar-equipped SOTAS (Stand-Off Target Acquisition System) aircraft in the early 1980s. Although similar in general concept to the French Army's Orchidée system currently being tested on a Super Puma helicopter (see page 74), development was curtailed and the equipment was not adopted for service.

Right: The black colouring and bristling antennas on the EH-60C increase its resemblance to a malevolent insect. The red object above the cabin is an IR jammer.

Below: Like all EW aircraft, the EH-60C is kept well away from prying eyes and inquisitive cameras. Few outsiders have been permitted a glimpse of its internal equipment.

Role: EW helicopter.
Length: 50ft 0.75in (15.26m).
Height: 16ft 10in (5.13m).
Rotor diameter: 53ft 8in (16.36m).
Weights — empty: c.12,400lb (5,600kg).
   Loaded: c.18,000lb (8,190kg).
   Max. takeoff: 20,250lb (9,185kg).
Powerplant(s): Two General Electric T700-GE-700 turboshafts.
Rating: 1,560shp (1,151kW).
Max. range: 324nm (600km) at max. take-off weight.
Max. speed: 160kts (296km/hr).
Ceiling: 10,400ft (3,170m).
Armament: None.

Yakovlev Yak-28R ''Brewer-D'' and -28E ''Brewer-E''

Two variants of the Yak-28 Brewer light bomber have been deployed in the reconnaissance and EW roles. The Yak-28R dedicated reconnaissance aircraft (designated Brewer D by NATO) was first deployed in the late 1960s. Immediately recognisable by its revised nose glazing, whose rear edge was sloped rather than vertical as on the bomber version, Brewer D had no weapons bay, the space probably being used for extra fuel, although some sources suggest that pallet-mounted cameras or SLARs may be installed. Profile of the dorsal radome has been modified, suggesting that a specialised radar may have replaced the J-band Short Horn navigation and bombing set. The aircraft has been seen carrying an elongated sensor pod almost directly beneath the bay area. Around 200 remain in service.

The Yak-28 ''Brewer E'' tactical EW aircraft is based on the now obsolete Brewer C light bomber, and those currently in

Above: The basic Yak-28 bomber is obsolescent. Most have been phased out, or in this case retired to a museum. Others were rebuilt as Brewer E EW aircraft.

Below: Features of the Brewer E include a nose radome (on some aircraft), a bulged entry hatch forward of the canopy, plus underwing chaff/flare dispensers.

Role: Tactical EW aircraft.
Length: 73ft 2in (22.3m).
Height: 12ft 11.5in (3.95m).
Wingspan: 42ft 6in (12.95m).
Weights — empty: c.22.000lb (10,000kg).
  Max. takeoff: c.42,000lb (19,000kg).
Powerplant(s): Two Tumanski R-11F turbojets.
Rating: 13,120lb (5,950kg) with A/B.
Tactical radius: c.485nm (900km) at altitude.
Max. speed: Mach 1.11 at altitude.
Ceiling: 55,000ft (16,750m).
Armament: None.

Above: This Brewer C bomber shows the glazed nose retained by many Brewer E, also the ventral radome for the Short Horn radar, a system not fitted to the EW variant.

service were probably created by the modification of existing bombers. Soviet designation of this aircraft could be Yak-28E, but this has never been confirmed.

Conversion of the aircraft for its new role involved deletion of the internal weapons bay and the ventral radome J-band Short Horn navigation and bombing radar. Most of the Brewer E aircraft sighted by Western observers retain the traditional Soviet glazed nose used on light bombers and given first-generation jet airliners, but some have been seen with a solid nose. It is not clear whether the latter represents a second variant, or if the entire fleet is being reworked to this standard.

Examination of the aircraft shows the presence of many antennas used by its on-board EW systems. Four are clustered around the extreme nose of aircraft which retain the nose glazing, and one on either side of the tailcone. Small teardrop fairings may be seen on either side of the fuselage, one beneath the cockpit, and two under the leading edge of the vertical fin. A prominent blade antenna is also mounted on the outer forward side of each engine nacelle.

Two prominent strakes beneath the belly run on either side of a prominent ventral canoe fairing through to house the antennas of powerful stand-off jammers. The location formerly used by the Short Horn radar now houses further EW kit, whose presence is betrayed by two small blade antennas. This could be system designed to jam NATO UHF communications.

Brewer E is also equipped to dispense chaff and flares. The aircraft retain the four underwing hardpoints of the bomber and recce versions. The inboard locations are used to carry fuel tanks, while the outboard are fitted with pods which may contain either chaff dispensers, or launch tubes for forward firing chaff rockets. Chaff/flare dispensers are thought to be incorporated in the front end of the belly strakes.

Like the original bomber versions, the Brewer D and E have never been cleared for export, so serve only with the Soviet Union. Estimates of the number of Brewer Es currently operational have ranged from 40 to 120 and the type is probably being slowly retired.

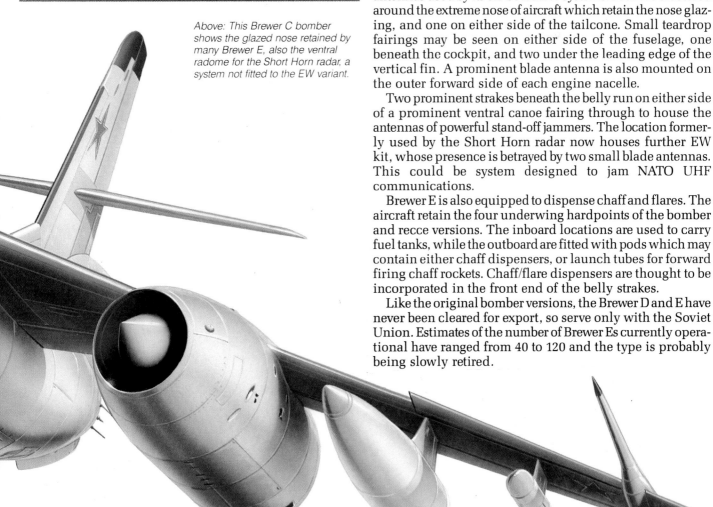

Aeritalia G.222VS

Having flown this tactical transport in 1970, and started production deliveries in 1976, Aeritalia looked for potential specialised uses for what is virtually a mini-Hercules.

The G.222VS (Versione Speciale) is an EW/elint aircraft. Recognisable by the presence of a small radome at the tip of the vertical fin, and a small thimble radome beneath the nose, this has a main cabin modified to house elint receivers, signal processors and recorders, plus a crew of up to ten EW operators. Flight deck crew is two, as on the transport. Up

to 40kW of electrical power is available for the mission avionics.

Only two examples of the G.222VS were built, the first of which made its maiden flight on 9 March 1978. These now serve with 71 Gruppo of the Italian Air Force, which also operates an EW version of the PD-808.

The next electronics variant to get off the drawing board was the G.222RM. Intended for radio/radar calibration duties, this flew for the first time in October 1982. Only four were built, and all still serve with an Italian Air Force calibration unit.

The only other specialised version to see service was the G.222SAA (Sistema Aeronautico Antincendio) firefighting

Right: A G.222VS taxies in at the end of a mission. Note the thimble radome under the nose, and the APU outlet just forward of the wheels in the port undercarriage sponson.

aircraft. Six were delivered to the Italian air force in the late 1970s.

Also in the late 1970s, Libya ordered the basic transport version, but a US trade embargo prevented the supply of T64 engines to that nation. To get around this problem, Aeritalia re-engined the aircraft with Rolls-Royce Tyne turboprops, creating the G.222T version. This was broadly similar in performance to the T64-engined model, the extra fuel burn of the UK engine being compensated for by the aircraft's higher cruising altitude. Range with full payload was increased from 740nm (1,370km) to 1,020nm (1,890km).

Libya bought only transports, designating these G.222L, but the extra power available from the new engines spurred the company to further studies of special-mission aircraft. Proposals were drawn up for new EW, drone-control, tanker, maritime-patrol, air-sea rescue, and airborne early-warning versions, also as a camera-equipped earth-resources photo-survey variant.

By the time that production of the G.222 ended in 1989, no orders had been received for any of these planned specialist versions. The basic transport model remains in service with the air forces of Italy (2 squadrons), Libya (20), Nigeria (5), Somalia (2), and Venezuela (6). Three supplied to the Argentine Army in 1977 are no longer in service, while the United Arab Emirates may have phased out the single example procured by Dubai in 1976.

Below: Compared with other elint types such as the RC-135, EP-3E and Il-20, the G.222VS has modestly sized antennas, which may indicate a less ambitious EW installation.

Role: EW aircraft.
Length: 74ft 5.5in (22.70m).
Height: 32ft 1.75in (9.80m).
Wingspan: 94ft 2in (28.70m).
Weights — empty: 32,165lb (14,590kg).
   Max. takeoff: 61,730lb (28,000kg).
Powerplant(s): Two General Electric T64-GE-P4D turboprops.
Rating: 3,400shp (2,535kW).
Max. range: 1,350nm (2,500km).
Max. speed: 291kts (540km/hr).
Ceiling: 25,000ft (7,620m).
Armament: None.

Above: This view of a parked G.222VS shows the circular radome at the top of the tailfin. Only two of these specialised aircraft were built, and both are still operational. This may seem a small fleet, but is typical of West European elint forces. For example, the UK built two of its Hawker Siddeley Nimrod R.1 elint aircraft (now rebuilt as R.2).

Boeing E-3A, B and C Sentry

Deliveries of this long-range AEW aircraft to the USAF started in March 1977, and the type became operational in April of the following year.

The first 24 production aircraft were E-3As, often referred to as the "core" version of the aircraft. These were equipped with the CC-1 computer, and nine situation display consoles. From the twenty-first aircraft onwards, the APY-1 radar was replaced by the improved APY-2.

The remaining 10 USAF aircraft were the "standard" version, with an APY-2 radar able to track maritime targets, also a faster CC-2 central computer with expanded memory, and improved communications. This was the version of the aircraft adopted by NATO.

1982 saw first deliveries to the NATO alliance. A fleet of 18 "standard" E-3As fly in NATO markings, and are officially registered as belonging to Luxembourg. Deliveries of five

Above: The Boeing 707 airframe gave US electronic engineers the space needed to install complex avionics, while leaving room for future upgrades. The E-3 Sentry is thus assured a long service career.

Left: A USAF E-3 fitted with CFM-56 engines? No, this is a Saudi Arabian Sentry in the temporary markings applied prior to delivery. The UK and France have also chosen the fuel-efficient CFM-65 for their E-3s.

examples of a CFM-56-powered variant to Saudi Arabia started in 1986.

Following the failure of a UK programme to create an AEW version of the BAe Nimrod, the Royal Air Force ordered six CFM-56-powered E-3A aircraft in February 1987, with deliveries due in 1991. RAF designation for the aircraft is Sentry AEW.1. Soon afterwards, France ordered three.

To upgrade the USAF fleet, Boeing has devised two modification kits — Block 20 for the ''core'' aircraft, and ''Block 25'' for the ''standard'' model. These are installed during scheduled maintenance sessions at Tinker AFB, Oklahoma.

Deliveries of the E-3B started in July 1984. Created by modifying existing E-3A ''core'' aircraft to Block 20 standard, these aircraft have the CC-2 computer, five more operator consoles, better communications, including JTIDS, plus hardpoints for chaff/flare dispensers. Earlier APY-1 radars on the first 20 aircraft built are upgraded to the -2 version.

The ten E-3A ''standard'' aircraft are being converted to the E-3C standard, receiving five more operator consoles, colour monitors, more radios, and the Have Quick A-Net secure communications system. The latter will also be installed on the RAF's aircraft.

In 1989, Westinghouse was given a $223 million USAF contract to begin full-scale development of a Radar System Improvement Programme (RSIP). Due to be flight tested in 1992-3, this will increase the sensitivity of the radar by replacing the current digital Doppler processor and radar data correlator with a new surveillance radar computer running software written in the Ada programming language. This will improve performance against low radar cross-section targets such as cruise missiles, and increase resistance to ECM. Range against most targets will be more than doubled. Flight testing of the improved radar is expected in the early 1990s, leading to a production decision in 1994.

Above: Although designed to warn against approaching aircraft, all but the earliest E-3s have radars able to track maritime targets.

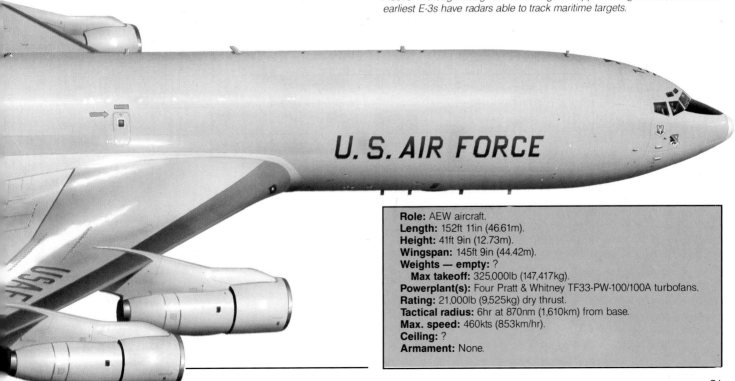

Role: AEW aircraft.
Length: 152ft 11in (46.61m).
Height: 41ft 9in (12.73m).
Wingspan: 145ft 9in (44.42m).
Weights — empty: ?
　Max takeoff: 325,000lb (147,417kg).
Powerplant(s): Four Pratt & Whitney TF33-PW-100/100A turbofans.
Rating: 21,000lb (9,525kg) dry thrust.
Tactical radius: 6hr at 870nm (1,610km) from base.
Max. speed: 460kts (853km/hr).
Ceiling: ?
Armament: None.

Grumman E-2C Hawkeye

In 1959 Grumman was given a contract to develop the E-2 AEW aircraft, while General Electric was ordered to develop the aircraft's APS-96 radar. The high-wing and twin-tail configuration of the new aircraft was similar to that of the piston-engined Grumman WF-2 Tracer which had just entered USN service, but the E-2 was a larger and heavier all-new design powered by turboprops rather than piston engines. The prototype which flew on 21 October 1960 carried no radar, but was fitted with the 24ft (7.3m) rotodome. A second prototype, the first to carry electronics, followed on 19 April 1961.

The new APS-96 radar used a then-new technique known as pulse compression. This involves electronically 'squeezing' a long radar pulse of the sort needed for good long-range detection performance in order to obtain synthetically the high range resolution obtained with short-duration pulses. As a result, the new radar had more than double the detection range from that of the Tracer's APS-82, locating targets at out to 200nm (362km).

EA-2A deliveries started in April 1964, and the aircraft became operational in the following year. From here on, the story of Hawkeye development is largely one of steadily improving radar technology. The APS-96 used as early E-2As quickly gave way to the APS-111, the first version to use AMTI.

The more powerful APS-120 (which offered a better capability when operating over land) was installed in the improved E-2C, along with the Litton ALR-73 passive target-detection system. This used four sets of antennas (mounted in the nose, tail and post and starboard wingtips) to detect radio or radar emissions from targets beyond the range of the APS-120.

The first of two pre-production aircraft flew for the first time on 20 January 1971, with the first production aircraft following on 23 September 1972. The E-2C entered USN service in November of the following year.

Radar improvements have continued, with the E-2C receiving the APS-125, followed by the APS-138 in the early 1980s, and most recently the APS-139. 1990 should see the service debut of the APS-145. Designed to overcome problems with

Above: An E-2C of VAW-127 starts engines prior to launch during operations off Libya on 16 March 1986. US air strikes were mounted against Libya a month later.

overland clutter, this set might eventually be retrofitted to the entire USN E-2C fleet. From 1988 onwards, aircraft coming off the production line were fitted with the uprated T56-A-427 engine.

Hawkeye has found a significant export role as a lower-cost alternative to the Boeing E-3 Sentry, and has now been adopted by the air arms of Egypt (5), Israel (4), Japan (11), and Singapore (4). The only problem in operating the type in this manner is limited range and endurance, both results of the aircraft's relatively small size and weight.

Normal mission endurance is 5.5 hours. When the UK evaluated the type in 1986 as a potential replacement for the unworkable Nimrod AEW.3, it was clear that the RAF requirement of six to seven hours on station at 750-1,000 miles (1,200-1,600km) from base could only be met by in-flight refuelling. Installation of an RAF-style refuelling probe would have posed few difficulties, but no space could be found within the cabin for a crew rest area.

Role: AEW aircraft.
Length: 57ft 6.75in (17.54m).
Height: 18ft 3.75in (5.58m).
Wingspan: 80ft 7in (24.56m).
Weights — empty: 38,063lb (17,265kg).
  Max. takeoff: 51,933lb (23,556kg).
Powerplant(s): Two Allison T56-A-425 turboprops.
Rating: 4,910shp (3,661kW).
Tactical radius: 3-4hr on station at 175nm (320km) from base.
Max. speed: 323kts (598km/hr).
Ceiling: 30,800ft (9,390m).
Armament: None.

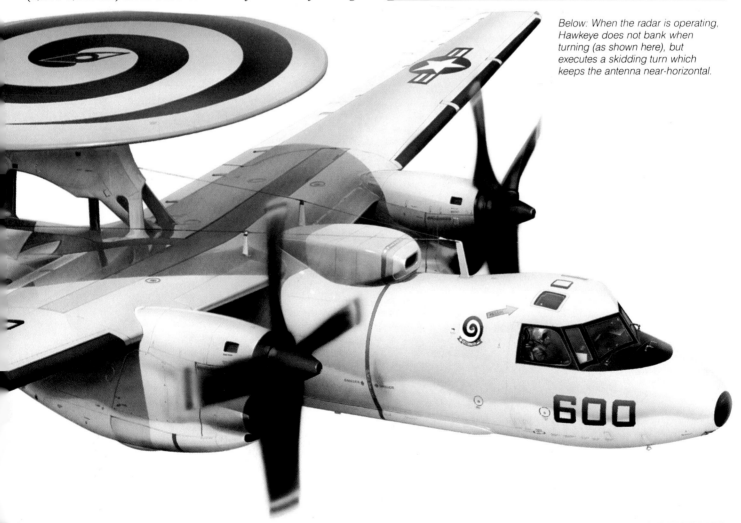

Below: When the radar is operating, Hawkeye does not bank when turning (as shown here), but executes a skidding turn which keeps the antenna near-horizontal.

Ilyushin "Mainstay"

When US spy satellites first detected an Il-76 Candid jet transport fitted with an E-3 style radome in the late 1970s, US intelligence expected that production and deployment of the type would swiftly follow. Deployment of the first aircraft was expected in 1983 or 1984 at the latest, with a fleet of at least 50 being operational by 1985-6. This was to prove unrealistic. As the UK and France have discovered with various national radar programmes, development of an effective long-range look-down radar can take longer than anticipated. By 1986 the Soviet Air Force had less than half a dozen Mainstays, although production was then running at around five examples a year.

Late in the following year, a Norwegian Air Force P-3 Orion operating over the Barents Sea encountered a Mainstay, and returned to base with clear photos of the new type. As anticipated from satellite imagery, the rotodome was located much further forward than on the Tu-126 or E-3. Its mast was almost directly above the wing trailing edge. A small E-4-style dorsal fairing mounted above the forward fuselage houses antennas used for satellite communications.

The IL-76 airframe has been modified for the new role, changes which have almost certainly warranted a new "Il-" type number, but this is not yet known. The fuselage has been extended in length, while the traditional glazed nose fitted to Soviet transports has been replaced by a new radome, and the aircraft retains the chin-mounted radome used on the transport to house a navigation/mapping radar. A small dark-coloured cylindrical fairing beneath the forward fuselage may house antennas for air-to-ground datalinks, while an air intake has been added at the base of the fin. A refuelling probe has been added to the upper surface of the nose.

Like the civil Il-76T and -76TD, Mainstay has no tail gun position. Its tail cone terminates in a small dark-coloured section which is probably the exhaust of an APU used to generate the massive amounts of electrical power needed by the radar and other avionics. If this is the case, the new air intake will be used to feed the APU, although it may also be associated with avionics cooling.

Little information has emerged on the radar system, other than its operating frequency of between 2.3 and 2.4GHz. US sources claim that it is able to detect low flying targets the size of cruise missiles. A new IFF system has been reported, and the aircraft is extensively equipped with EW equipment, most of which is probably ESM gear intended to detect targets at beyond radar range, or to allow the aircraft to operate in passive mode. Small fairings on either side of the front and rear fuselage probably house the ESM antennas. Similar fairings may be seen on the Il-76M and -76MD versions of the military transport.

Maximum range of the basic Il-76 transport is around 4,100 miles (6,600km). At a normal cruising speed of 400-430kts (750-800km/hr), this suggests an endurance in the AEW role of up to eight hours. This can obviously be extended by air refuelling.

A tanker version of the basic Il-76 has now been developed. Codenamed "Midas", it has been in service since 1987.

Role: AEW aircraft.
Length: 185ft (56.4m).
Wingspan: 167ft (50.9m).
Weights — empty: c.165,000lb? (75,000kg?).
 Max. takeoff: 375,000lb (170,100kg).
Powerplant(s): Four Soloviev D-30KP turbofans.
Rating: 26,455lb (12,000kg) dry thrust.
Max. speed: c.400kts (750km/hr).
Armament: None.

Above: This new photo of a "Mainstay" clearly shows that the tailcone is not an exhaust (as suggested in the text), but a small radome, probably for EW systems.

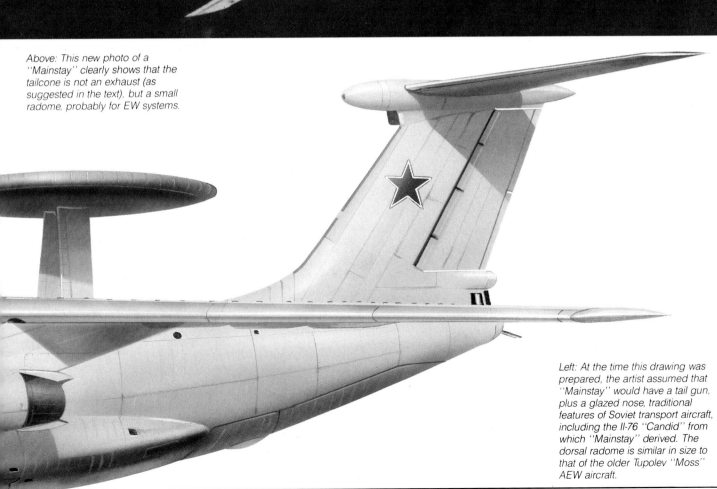

Left: At the time this drawing was prepared, the artist assumed that "Mainstay" would have a tail gun, plus a glazed nose, traditional features of Soviet transport aircraft, including the Il-76 "Candid" from which "Mainstay" derived. The dorsal radome is similar in size to that of the older Tupolev "Moss" AEW aircraft.

Beriev Be-12 Chaika

At first sight, the Beriev Chaika (known to NATO as "Mail") looks like an anachronism. The West has long since written off flying boats and amphibians as a military aircraft, yet the long-established Beriev bureau has designed little else. The Be-12 was developed to meet a 1957 specification for an amphibian able to replace the piston-engined Be-6, a type which by then had been in service for about seven years.

Georgii Beriev had studied jet-powered flying boats, flying the twin-jet model R-1 in 1952. He may have decided to build rival jet and turboprop designs to meet the new requirement. The Be-12 amphibian flown for the first time probably in 1960 had a straight wing and two Ivchenko AI-20D turboprops, while the Be-10 (which probably flew in the follow-ing year) was a pure flying boat with a swept wing and two Lyulka AL-7RV engines.

In 1961 the Be-10 established several speed and altitude records, but was not accepted for production. Probably less than half a dozen prototypes were built. Development of the less ambitious Be-12 moved slowly, but production deliveries began in 1964, and more than 200 were built.

The presence of a magnetic anomaly detector (MAD) "sting" aft of the tail confirms that the aircraft was originally built with the ASW mission in mind. The aircraft has a crew of six — pilot, co-pilot, navigator, electronics operator and two ASW systems operators. A weapons bay is located in the rear fuselage, while the tail houses sonobuoy launchers and the auxiliary power unit which provides electrical power for the avionics. Air-to-surface rockets and other stores can be carried on underwing hardpoints outboard of the propellor discs.

Role: ASW/recce flying boat.
Length: 101ft 6.5in (30.95m).
Height: ?
Wingspan: 97ft 5.75in (29.71m).
Weights — empty: c.40.000lb (18,000kg).
   Loaded: 65,000lb (29,500kg).
Powerplant(s): Two Ivchenko AI-20D turboprops.
Rating: 4,190shp (3,124kW).
Max. range: 2,150nm (4,000km).
Max. speed: 328kts (608km/hr).
Ceiling: 40,000ft (12,000m).
Armament: Torpedoes, depth charges and other stores.

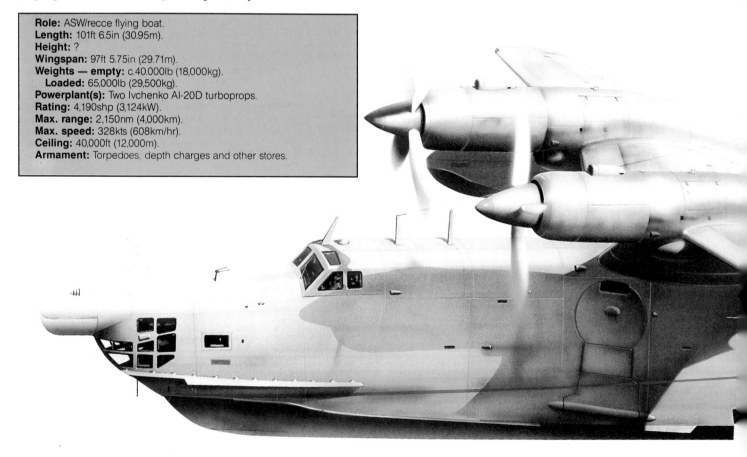

Other roles include maritime-patrol and anti-ship, and at least one EW version has been reported. Limited avionics updating has taken place, with some aircraft receiving a new nose radar, a tail-warning system, and ESM receivers.

With the arrival of the Il-38 ''May'', the Be-12 may have been gradually relegated to secondary roles such as coastal patrol and fishery-protection. Since the early 1980s, the number in service seems to have stayed constant at an estimated 75-90, suggesting either a very low attrition rate, or a good supply of aircraft in storage. The Be-12 was never exported. Those seen in Egyptian markings during the early 1970s were Soviet-crewed.

The Be-12 may also have been the inspiration for China's Harbin SH-5 flying boat. First flown in 1976, this is a larger aircraft powered by four 3,150shp (2,349kW) Shanghai WJ-5A-1 turboprops. Its wing may have been derived from that of the Y-8 (An-12) transport.

Above: Both Ivchenko AI-20D engines running at full-power, and wingtip floats already clear of the sea surface, a Be-12 of the Black Sea Fleet is about to take off.

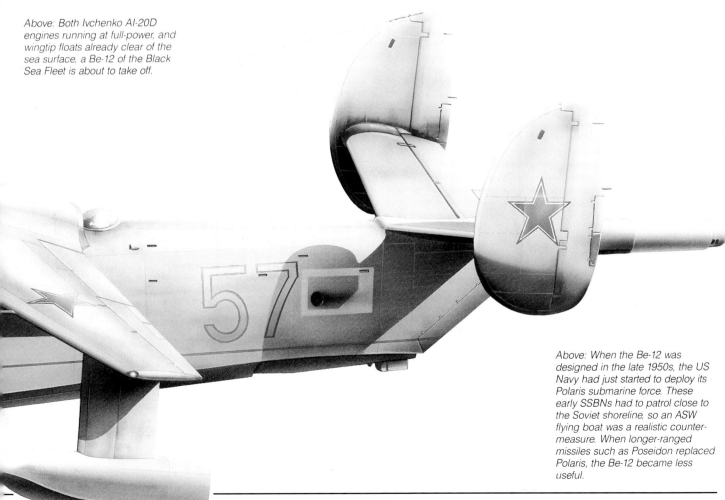

Above: When the Be-12 was designed in the late 1950s, the US Navy had just started to deploy its Polaris submarine force. These early SSBNs had to patrol close to the Soviet shoreline, so an ASW flying boat was a realistic countermeasure. When longer-ranged missiles such as Poseidon replaced Polaris, the Be-12 became less useful.

Ilyushin Il-38 "May"

First flown in 1957, the Il-18 four-engined long-range transport entered service with Aeroflot in April 1959. A production run of around 800 examples followed at the GAZ-30 aircraft plant, ending around 1970. By this time, the line had switched to the Il-38 maritime-patrol variant, known to NATO as "May".

In drawing up its new design, the Ilyushin team retained the wings, tail undercarriage and engines of the airliner, but probably carried out some minor redesign work and restress

ing in order to toughen the structure for the over-water role, and to improve corrosion resistance. The presence of a heavy electronics bay in the windowless forward fuselage unbalanced the aircraft, forcing the designers to reposition the wing and restress the fuselage. On the Il-18, the wing had been mounted about half way down the length of the fuselage, but on the Il-38 it is located much further forward.

Two weapons bays were added, one ahead of the wing box, the other aft of the wing. These are fitted with outward-hinging doors, and are used to carry the aircraft's armament and sonobuoys. On the Il-18D long-ranger version of the airliner, these locations housed fuel cells. Weaponry is pro-

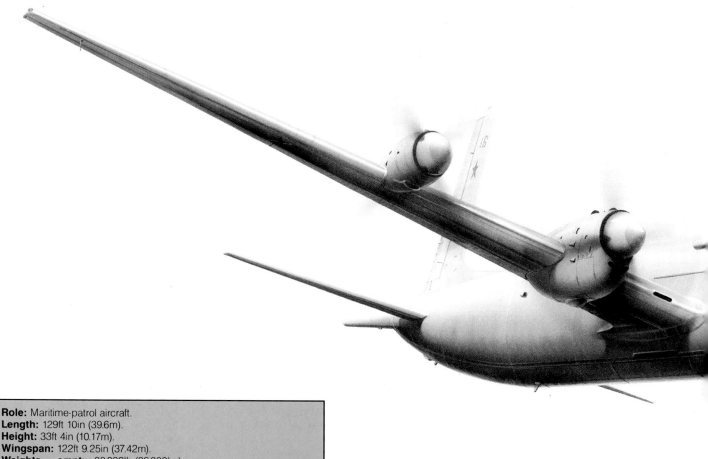

Role: Maritime-patrol aircraft.
Length: 129ft 10in (39.6m).
Height: 33ft 4in (10.17m).
Wingspan: 122ft 9.25in (37.42m).
Weights — empty: 80,000lb (36,000kg).
   Max. takeoff: 140,000lb (64,000kg).
Powerplant(s): Four Ivchenko AI-24M turboprops.
Rating: 4,250shp (3,169kW).
Max. range: 3,887nm (7,200km).
Max. speed: 347kts (645km/hr).
Ceiling: c.33,000ft (10,000m).
Armament: Torpedoes, depth charges, and other stores.

bably confined to homing torpedoes and depth bombs; earlier reports of underwing hardpoints for anti-ship missiles are probably incorrect. Nuclear depth bombs are probably available for wartime use, but like other Soviet nuclear weapons will be stored under KGB rather than military control.

Operating frequency of the "Wet Eye" surface search radar is in J-band, a high frequency which will maximise the angular resolution of the antenna and help reduce the effects of sea 'clutter' in the radar returns. The tail-mounted MAD is an obvious feature, and some observers interpret a tiny chin fairing aft of the aircraft's nose-mounted naviga-tion/search/weather radar to be the housing for an EO sensor.

Several small antennas distributed around the airframe are probably part of the aircraft's ESM suite. One may be found at each wingtip, another on top of the vertical fin, and a fourth under the lower fuselage.

Total production has involved about 70 aircraft, most of which serve with Soviet Naval Aviation. Sole export customer has been India, which ordered three in 1975 to re-equip INAS 315. These aircraft were delivered in 1977. A total of five are now in service. The crew is though to number 12 — pilot, co-pilot and engineer on the flight deck and nine at tactical stations in the fuselage.

Right: An F-14 Tomcat of VF-111 escorts an Il-38 away from US Navy surface forces. This photo gives a good view of the aircraft MAD "sting" and "Wet Eye" radar.

Below: Any NATO submarine commander who gets this view of an Il-38 through his periscope would be wise to dive deep, run silent, and listen out for newly dropped sonobuoys.

Lockheed S-3B and ES-3A Viking

Designed to replace the Grumman S-2, this carrier-based ASW aircraft entered service in 1973. A total of 187 S-3As was delivered until production ended in 1978. The Viking is equipped to a high standard, with sonobuoy systems, FLIR, MAD tail boom, radar, ECM and ESM equipment packed into the compact airframe. The sole operator is the US Navy, although Canada operates the same avionics in its CP-140 Aurora derivative of the P-3 Orion. A total of 40 USN S-3As is now being converted to the -3B standard, receiving an improved APS-137(V)1 radar, ARR-78 sonobuoy receiving system, UYS-1 Proteus acoustic processor, and provision for Harpoon anti-ship missiles, a GPS satnav system, and the JTIDS communication system. The first of two S-3B prototypes flew in the mid-1980s, and the first production S-3B was delivered in December 1987. A total of 160 may eventually be modified.

By the mid-1980s, the US Navy urgently needed a replacement for the elderly Douglas EA-3 Skywarrior carrier-based elint aircraft, but by the spring of 1987 it became obvious that the funds needed to buy new airframes were not available. Instead, it was decided to withdraw from service 16 S-3A Vikings (the equivalent of almost two squadrons) and have these airframes rebuilt for the elint task.

In the spring of 1988 Lockheed was given a $66 million contract to build two prototypes of the proposed ES-3A elint aircraft. The first would be an aerodynamic prototype intended to check the effects of the new antennas and other modifications. The second would be a working EW aircraft.

The weapon bay is not required in the new role, so its doors are removed and replaced by cheek fairings which can be opened on the ground to give access to the avionics. The 61 sonobuoy tubes in the rear lower fuselage are also removed, and the area reskinned.

A long dorsal spine has been added, and has at its front end a radome covering an omni-directional receiver antenna, while two smaller radomes and 35 other antennas bristle from the fuselage. The drag of these fittings is expected to raise fuel consumption by a few per cent, and add several knots to the landing speed.

The on-board elint systems are off-the-shelf equipment as used on the larger Lockheed EP-3 elint variants of the P-3 Orion. If the test and evaluation programme runs according to schedule, conversions of S-3A airframes to ES-3A configuration will be completed by late 1992.

Like the basic ASW version, the aircraft has a crew of four — pilot, EW co-ordinator and two EW operators — all of whom have ejection seats. The flying controls have been removed from the right-hand cockpit seat. Operation of the on-board systems will normally be under the control of the crew, but the equipment can also be controlled from surface fitted with the new Battle Group Passive Horizon Extension System (BGPHES).

Role: Carrier-borne ASW aircraft/carrier borne elint aircraft.
Length: 53ft 4in (16.62m).
Height: 22ft 9in (6.93m).
Wingspan: 68ft 8in (20.93m).
Weights — empty: 26,554lb (12,044kg).
  Loaded: 43,491lb (19,727kg).
Powerplant(s): Two General Electric TF34-GE-2 turbofans.
Rating: 9,280lb (4,210kg) dry thrust.
Max. range: 3,040nm (5,630km).
Max. speed: 440kts (815km/hr) at sea level.
Ceiling: 35,000ft (10,670kg).
Armament: Torpedoes, depth charges, and underwing Harpoon antiship missiles.

Above left: The latest variant of the S-3 Viking to take to the skies is the ES-3A. A mass of external antennas and aerials indicate this model's specialised Electronic Intelligence (elint) gathering capabilities which the US Navy plans to maximise during the 1990s.

Left: Most obvious sign of the rebuild programme which converted US Navy E-3A Viking to the new S-3B standard is the presence of an AGM-84 Harpoon anti-ship missile under the wing. The same rebuild also greatly improved the radar and acoustic-processing systems.

Tupolev Tu-22 "Blinder C"

As the Tu-16 Badger bomber entered service in the mid 1950s studies of a potential replacement were already under way. Thinking ran along similar lines to that of its Western design offices: speed and height were seen as the keys to survival. The logical replacement for a bomber designed to fly at high subsonic speed was thought to be a supersonic design able to cruise at still higher altitudes.

The goal set for the Tupolev bureau was the creation of an aircraft in the same weight class as Badger, but capable of covering the ground at a much higher speed. The end result was an aircraft 20 per cent heavier than Badger, but with about 7 per cent less tactical radius even when flown in fuel-saving subsonic flight. Use of afterburning took the aircraft to Mach 1.4 at best, well below the B-58's Mach 2, but carved forty to fifty per cent off the aircraft's tactical radius.

The prototype TU-22 probably flew in 1959, but by that time Western Europe had already flown supersonic intercepters such as the Mirage III and Lightning. Since these were much faster than the new Soviet bomber, the latter's usefulness as a long-range penetrating bomber armed with free-falling weapons was obviously limited. Total production of the initial Blinder A bomber version may have been restricted to the nine aircraft which took part in the 1961 Tushino air display.

It was quickly followed by the missile-armed Blinder B, which carried a single AS-4 Kitchen on the centreline. At least 170 were built for the Soviet Air Force in the 1960s. Surplus aircraft (stripped of their missiles and nuclear-delivery systems) were supplied to Iraq (12) and Libya (24) during the 1970s. Both customers used the type in action, Iraq using them against Kurdish guerillas, and Libya sending several to Uganda to combat the Tanzanian invasion which toppled the Amin regime. Libyan Blinders also supported that nation's invasion of Chad until a French Hawk battery demonstrated the

Below: The missile-armed "Blinder B" rapidly replaced the original "Blinder A", an aircraft built in small numbers and armed only with free-falling bombs.

type's vulnerability in 1987 by downing one of a formation of two attempting to raid the Chadian capital.

Naval Aviation was less interested in Blinder than the Air Force, taking delivery of only 60 examples of the Blinder C reconnaissance aircraft. These now serve with the Baltic fleet. Most retain the nose radome of the earlier versions, and presumably the same Down Beat radar, but a non-standard radome has been reported on at least one aircraft. The variations in the location of blade antennas and dielectric fairings on different aircraft suggest that several Blinder C sub-variants have been created for specific operational tasks.

The final member of the series was the Blinder D conversion trainer, which had a second canopy for the instructor above and behind the pilot. At least one variable-geometry Blinder is reported to have flown in the late 1960s, and a small batch may have been built. Their designation Tu-22M may have been passed for political reasons to the later Tupolev Backfire. Also unconfirmed is the reported existence of a long-range interceptor version developed to replace the Tu-128 Fiddler.

Above: Blinder was probably the most visually attractive Soviet jet bomber, but good looks were not matched with the performance needed to ensure a long production run.

Role: Maritime reconnaissance/elint a/c.
Length: 132ft 11.5in (40.53m).
Height: 35ft 0in (10.67m).
Wingspan: 78ft 0in (23.75m).
Weights — empty: c.88,000lb (40,000kg).
  Max. takeoff: 185,000lb (84,000kg).
Powerplant(s): Two Koliesov VD-7 turbojets.
Rating: c.31,000lb (14,000kg) with A/B.
Tactical radius: 1,670nm (3,100km).
Max. speed: Mach 1.4 at altitude.
Ceiling: c.60,000ft (18,300m).
Armament: None.

Left: By studying the antennas and dielectric fairings of different aircraft, Western analysts have identified at least five subvariants of the "Blinder C" recce version. All have the prominent antenna fairing seen on this example under the fuselage beneath the cockpit, and retain some of the semicircle of transparencies around the nose.

A book of this size cannot fully cover all of the major jet and turboprop-powered aircraft currently used or under development for the reconnaissance and EW roles. Those described in detail were chosen to represent a cross-section of the aircraft currently used. The other main types are described below.

Aérospatiale AS.532 Orchidée

France's Orchidée (Observatoire Radar Cohérent Héliporté d'Investigation des Eléments Ennemis) system is based on the Aérospatiale AS.532 Super Puma Mk2 helicopter. An X-band radar antenna mounted beneath the rear of the cabin provides coverage of terrain out to around 90 miles (150km) in all weathers. Developed by LCTAR, the radar is a frequency-agile pulse-Doppler unit designed to detect ground vehicles and low-flying helicopters.

The French Army appreciates the vulnerability of helicopters flying near the front line. The helicopter would normally operate more than 20 miles (32km) back from the FEBA. It would not be on continuous patrol, but will use its radar to take brief "snapshots" which can be relayed to the ground via a datalink. In combat the radar will be turned on for periods of probably less than a minute before shutting down while the aircraft is repositioned prior to making another scan of the battle area. The downlink (which is codenamed Agatha) can transmit the results of a single scan in less than 10 seconds, allowing detailed analysis.

Antonov An-74 "Madcap"

The Antonov bureau developed two prototypes of this medium-sized AEW aircraft using its An-74 Coaler STOL transport as a starting point. Flight trials were first reported in the winter of 1987-8. The most novel feature of the design is the location of the radome, on the top of a forward swept vertical tail fin. This is about half the diameter of the Flat Jack installation on the Tu-126 Moss. The range will be reduced accordingly, but this is not so important for an aircraft presumably intended to operate from tactical air bases much closer to the front line than the sort of airfield which would support operations of the larger Ilyushin Il-76 Mainstay.

ASTOR

Britain's joint Army/RAF Area STand-Off Radar (ASTOR) programme involves two different radars, both developed by Thorn-EMI. One is a pulse-Doppler set being test flown in a Pilatus Britten-Norman Turbo Islander twin-turboprop light aircraft. Developed to meet the needs of the Army, it is intended to track ground vehicles, allowing troop and vehicle concentrations to be identified for attack. The RAF is more interested in detecting static targets such as fuel or ammunition dumps, and the radar developed to meet its requirement is a synthetic-aperture unit test flown in an obsolete Canberra light bomber.

A requirement for 12 suitably configured aircraft is envisaged, although the changing military and political situation in Europe may in time have an influence on the future of the entire project.

Below: Orchidée radar on flight test under Aérospatiale Puma trials aircraft.

Below: The ASTOR Islander camouflaged in Army Air Corps colours.

Antonov An-12 "Cub-B", C and D

Between 10 and 20 Cub-B elint versions of the An-12 tactical transport serve with the Soviet Navy, operating in support of the Baltic and Black Sea fleets. Some are sent on overseas deployment — Cub-Bs have been seen over the Indian Ocean. These aircraft often operate in civil markings, and some have the guns removed from the tail position. Most carry an extensive array of blade and stub antennas on the lower fuselage or cabin roof, while others have been sighted carrying radomes of various types in addition to the chin radome covering the ubiquitous I-band Toadstool navigation/mapping radar.

Operational since the early 1970s, the Antonov An-12 Cub-C was one of the first Soviet dedicated jamming aircraft to carry power-managed jammers. Palletised jamming equipment reported to cover "at least five wavebands" are located beneath the floor of the main cabin, along with dispensers for chaff and flares. It has since been joined by the Cub-D, a version fitted with an alternative jamming installation. The joint C and D fleet is thought to number around 30.

Above: This "Cub C" is used for elint eavesdropping tasks.

Boeing/Grumman E-8B JSTARS

From 1997 onwards the USAF hopes to deploy a fleet of at least 20 aircraft fitted with a sideways looking radar able to peer up to 125 miles (200km) over the NATO front line, recording the movements of ground vehicles and slow-flying helicopters. The E-8B is based on ex-airline JT3D-powered 707-300C airliners rebuilt for the new role. The USAF would have liked all-new airframes, but the 707/E-3/E-6 line is due to close in the early 1990s.

Two E-8A prototypes flown in the late 1980s will be supplemented by a third, which will eventually be delivered as one of the production aircraft. During the trials in which the prototypes flew off the east coast of Florida, the Norden radar contained in the 26ft long (7.9m) underfuselage fairing was able to record road traffic on local highways, and vehicle targets at Eglin AFB.

Radar data will be transmitted via an omnidirectional secure data link to USAF and US Army commanders, while up to 15 Motorola AN/TSQ-132 ground stations mounted on wheeled vehicles will be able simultaneously to send to the aircraft requests for additional information, such as examination of a new ground area of interest, or re-examination of a previous area.

Below: The antenna fairing beneath the E-8 contains the JSTARS radar antenna.

British Aerospace Nimrod MR.2P and R.1P

The first two prototypes flew in 1967 and were based on Comet airframes. The first production Nimrod MR.1 maritime-patrol aircraft flew on 28 June 1968, and the type entered front-line service with 201 Squadron in 1970. Five squadrons operated the type, one of which was disbanded in 1979 to make airframes available for the AEW programme.

Service career of the MR.1 was relatively short. In 1975 work began on converting 31 aircraft to the much-improved MR.2 standard. (One of the original 46 had been lost in an accident, three had been built to AEW.3 standard while a further 11 were earmarked for AEW conversion.)

In addition to the 46 aircraft originally procured, the RAF also received three Nimrod R.1s. Recognisable by the absence of a tail boom, these were issued to 51 Squadron at Wyton for use as elint platforms. They have since been rebuilt to the R.2 standard. A proposed mid-life update of the MR.2 was abandoned in 1990 due to a re-estimate of remaining airframe life.

Below: A BAe Nimrod R.1P operated by No. 51 Squadron, RAF.

Dassault-Breguet Atlantic

Construction of this twin-turboprop aircraft was carried out by an international consortium known as SECBAT (Société d'Etudes et de Construction du Breguet ATlantic). This was made up of Aérospatiale and Breguet (France), Dornier, MBB and VFW (West Germany), Aeritalia (Italy), Fokker, SABCA and Sonaca (the Netherlands), while the engines and propellors were produced by Rolls-Royce and British Aerospace (UK), Snecma and Ratier (France), MAN (Germany) and FN (Belgium). By the time that production ended in 1974, the group had built 87 aircraft, with deliveries to France (40), Germany (20), Italy (18) and the Netherlands (9). Three Aeronavale aircraft were re-sold to Pakistan in the mid-1970s.

West Germany updated its fleet in the early 1980s, replacing the radar, ESM, tape recorder and sonobuoy ejection system with new equipments of higher performance, modifying the acoustic processing system to incorporate digital signal processing, and installing an INS. These modifications should allow the aircraft to remain in service until the mid-1990s. West Germany originally bought five Atlantics which were fitted out for the elint role, and the four survivors are still in operation over the Baltic.

Although generally similar to the older aircraft (known as Atlantic 1), the Atlantic 2 now being built for the French Navy has an all-new avionics suite based around a digital data bus, and including a SAT/TRT FLIR sensor in a steerable chin turret, a Thomson-CSF Iguane I-band search radar, and a Thomson-CSF Sadang acoustic-processing system.

Dassault-Breguet Mirage III, 5, 50 and 2000

From the start of the programme, Dassault envisaged the Mirage III as a family of warplanes. The full-scale production contract awarded in October 1958 for Mirage IIIC interceptors was to be followed by orders for other variants — the IIIB and IIID two-seat trainers, the IIIE fighter-bomber, and the IIIR reconnaissance aircraft.

To accommodate the camera installation, the nose of the IIIR was extended. Unlike the IIIE, it retained the navigation system of the IIIC, so enjoyed a swifter development. The first production example flew for the first time on 1 February 1963, almost a year ahead of the strike equivalent.

The initial French Air Force contract for reconnaissance aircraft covered a batch of 50 IIIRs, and was followed by an order for 20 of the improved IIIRD model. The first overseas customer for the reconnaissance version was South Africa, which took delivery of four IIIRZs during the winter of 1966-7.

France initially deployed the improved 2000 in the 2000C interceptor and 2000B trainer versions, with most export customers specifying similar fighter and trainer models. Any French plans for a reconnaissance model are as yet unspecified, with the 2000N and 2000E versions for nuclear and conventional strike taking precedence. Sole customer for a recce 2000 was Abu Dhabi, which has three 2000RADs, but the aircraft is still offered for export.

Below: Mirage 5BR of No. 42 Squadron, Belgian Air Force.

Grumman EA-6B Prowler

This shipboard EW aircraft was created in the mid-1960s by stretching the fuselage of the A-6 Intruder to make room for two extra crewmen, then installing an ALQ-99 jamming system. The aircraft flew for the first time on 25 May 1968, and entered service with the US Navy in 1971, replacing the two-seat EA-6A. Most current service aircraft are the ICAP-2 standard. This has an EW suite able to deal with all the emitters in a typical air-defence complex, and can carry AGM-88 Harm anti-radiation missiles. Flight trials of the ADVCAP (ADVanced CAPability) version of the aircraft began in 1988. This will remain the standard version until production ends in 1992.

Below: US Navy EA-6B Prowler in low-visibility markings.

Grumman OV-1D and RV-1D Mohawk

The US Army still operates more than 100 examples of the twin-turboprop Mohawk reconnaissance and observation aircraft. Most are OV-1Ds, which can carry optical cameras, or elint equipment, plus an optional UAS-4 IR linescanner or an APS-94 sideways looking radar. Around 20 Mohawks are the RV-1D elint version, which carries the ALQ-133 Quick Look II, an elint suite whose functions are now being taken over by the Guardrail Common Sensor suite in the Beech RC-12K. Israel still has six RV-1Ds.

Below: The pencil-like radome beneath this OV-10D is for the APS-94 radar.

Lockheed P-3 Orion

This long-established maritime-patrol aircraft has been progressively updated to cope with new types of submarine. The original P-3A entered service in 1962, and was followed by the P-3B in 1966, then the P-3C in 1969. A series of avionics retrofits have been applied to the P-3C. Latest is the Update IV. Intended to counter the latest generation of quiet Soviet submarines such as the Sierra class (which emits only 1/20 the noise of previous-generation Soviet SSNs). This version of the aircraft will be a rebuild of 80 P-3C Update II aircraft, adding the APS-137 radar, AAS-36 infra-red detection set, a new UYS-2 acoustic processor able to handle signals from up to 54 sonobuoys simultaneously, an ALR-66(V)5 ESM system, satellite communications, NavStar/GPS navigation, greater data-processing capability, and better crew workstations.

The P-7, originally known as the P-3G, is due to fly for the first time in late 1991. Around 6.5ft (2m) longer than the P-3, and driven by General Electric GE83 turboprops, it offers twice the payload of the P-3C and incorporates 78 major changes to the basic P-3 design. The USN takes deliveries from 1991.

Below: P-3C Orion of the Royal Netherlands Air Force.

Myasishchev ''Mystic'' (RAM-M)

Originally designated RAM-M by US intelligence, this high-altitude reconnaissance aircraft was first reported in 1982. Originally attributed to the Yakovlev design bureau, it is a product of the former Myasishchev bureau, now part of the Molniya Scientific Enterprise.

In appearance the aircraft can best be described as a U-2 whose aft fuselage and tail have been amputated and replaced by a twin-boom assembly similar to that on Rockwell OV-10 Bronco.

Development has been protracted. The first two prototypes were single-engined, but a twin-engined variant has now flown. If successful, the latter configuration could be selected for a production batch.

Sukhoi Su-24 ''Fencer''—E and F

Fencer E is the first dedicated reconnaissance model of this Soviet variable-geometry fighter-bomber. Developed for Naval Aviation, it carries an internal sensor suite, and can also be used to deliver anti-ship missiles. Little is known about this version, and details of a reported Fencer F are even sketchier. The latter is thought to be an EW aircraft designed to replace the Yak-28 Brewer-E in the escort and stand-off jamming roles.

Tupolev Tu-95/Tu-142 ''Bear''

Current reconnaissance models of this obsolete turboprop-powered strategic bomber are the Bear D, E and F. Bear D was the first to carry the huge 100 mile (160km) range I-band Big Bulge radar, whose antenna is located inside a huge ventral radome directly under the wings, and was designed to operate from non-Warsaw Pact airfields. From 1970 onwards, the type was sighted operating from bases such as San Antonio de los Banos (Cuba), Conakry (Guinea), Belas (Angola), Cam Ranh Bay (Vietnam), plus airfields in Ethiopia and Libya.

In the late 1960s, the Tupolev bureau started work on a major revision of the aircraft intended to make it more suitable for the reconnaissance role. These new features were sufficiently drastic to warrant a new designation of Tu-142.

A redesigned wing incorporates a simpler structure, complete with rear-ranged tanks of slightly increased capacity, and double-slotted flaps replacing the earlier plain flaps. Other externally visible changes included extended nacelles on the inboard engines (probably to reduce drag), an extended front fuselage incorporating a plug of around 5ft 9in (1.75m), and a larger rudder designed to offset the increased side area of the new front fuselage. Further versions could be fielded in the 1990s.

Above: The Tu-95 ''Bear D'' was the maritime recce version of the Tupolev bomber.

Tupolev Tu-126 ''Moss''

In 1968 the Soviet Union released a documentary film which gave the West its first glimpse of the Soviet Air Force's first — and until recently only — airborne early-warning aircraft. Boeing was not to receive a development contract for what would become the E-3 until 1970, but here was what looked like a Soviet equivalent flying a decade ahead of the planned IOC of the US aircraft.

At first sight, it seemed like the days of Sputniks, Luniks and Yuri Gagarin revisited, with the Soviet Union displaying an apparent technological superiority, but any feelings of panic in high places must have been swiftly allayed by the realisation that there was no way that the Soviet electronics industry could have carved a decade off the development time needed to create an effective next-generation AEW aircraft. The new aircraft had to be viewed not as a Soviet AWACS but as a long-range equivalent of Western types such as the early-1960s Grumman Hawkeye.

The Tu-114 was a near-ideal basis for the new aircraft. Its close relationship with the Tu-95 Bear bomber assured the user of an existing pool of trained manpower and spares, while its 13ft (4m) diameter fuselage offered more internal volume than the slimmer fuselage of the Bear. Since most of the avionics were probably based on vacuum tube technology, space was at a premium.

Only seven of the original 20 aircraft built now remain in service.

Below: Despite its size, the Tu-126 ''Moss'' was of limited effectiveness.

Westland Sea King AEW.2

During the 1982 Falklands War, Westland and Thorn-EMI swiftly created the two prototypes of the AEW Sea King. To house the new radar antenna, a kettledrum-shaped inflatable and pressurised radome made from Kevlar-impregnated fabric was devised. Located on a swivelling mount, this could be lowered into the horizontal position by a hydraulic mechanism once the aircraft was airborne. Two Thorn-EMI Searchwater radars were hastily modified to improve clutter rejection in the new role, then mounted in the aircraft. Eleven weeks after work had started, the equipment was installed, tested, commissioned, and ready for service. Embarked aboard the newly completed carrier *Illustrious*, they headed for the Falklands in August 1982.

As the risk of further military confrontation in the South Atlantic faded, the Sea King AEWs were withdrawn from service. Their hasty development had left many ''rough edges'' which, although acceptable in wartime, needed to be engineered out of a fully-fledged system. On 9 November 1984, the original two Mk2 AEW aircraft (now duly updated) were delivered back to the Royal Navy, forming the first equipment of 849 Squadron of RNAS Culdrose. By August of the following year, the unit's A Flight was in service aboard *Illustrious*, restoring the RN AEW ''umbrella''. A fleet of 10 Sea Kings now serves with 849 Squadron, which provides three-aircraft flights for shipboard deployment.

Below: Westland AEW.2 Sea King with antenna in the deployed position.

Index